Socialism for Soloists

Dedicated to the Ernies of the world

Socialism for Soloists

Spelling Out the Social Contract

William A. Edmundson

polity

First published in 2021 by Polity Press

Polity Press
65 Bridge Street
Cambridge CB2 1UR, UK

Polity Press
101 Station Landing
Suite 300
Medford, MA 02155, USA

ISBN-13: 978-1-5095-4182-9
ISBN-13: 978-1-5095-4183-6 (pb)

A catalogue record for this book is available from the British Library.
Library of Congress Cataloging-in-Publication Data

Names: Edmundson, William A. (William Atkins), 1948- author.
Title: Socialism for soloists : spelling out the social contract / William A. Edmundson.
Description: Cambridge, UK ; Medford, MA, USA : Polity Press, 2021. | Includes bibliographical references and index. | Summary: "Why sturdy individualists should support socialism, not capitalism"-- Provided by publisher.
Identifiers: LCCN 2020046519 (print) | LCCN 2020046520 (ebook) | ISBN 9781509541829 (hardback) | ISBN 9781509541836 (paperback) | ISBN 9781509541843 (epub)
Subjects: LCSH: Socialism. | Justice. | Equality.
Classification: LCC HX73 .E33 2021 (print) | LCC HX73 (ebook) | DDC 335--dc23
LC record available at https://lccn.loc.gov/2020046519
LC ebook record available at https://lccn.loc.gov/2020046520

Typeset in 11 on 13 Sabon
by Fakenham Prepress Solutions, Fakenham, Norfolk NR21 8NL
Printed and bound in Great Britain by TJ Books Ltd, Padstow, Cornwall

For further information on Polity, visit our website:
politybooks.com

Contents

Acknowledgments

The ideas presented here evolved from discussions with members of my Theories of Justice seminars at Georgia State University. I thank Leslie Wolf for enabling me to block off the time I needed to transform these ideas into book form.

Portions of Chapter 5 appeared as "What Are the Means of Production?" in *The Journal of Political Philosophy* 28(4), 2020, pp. 421–37

I owe a special debt of gratitude to my editor, George Owers, and to two anonymous referees for Polity Books.

The essential idea is that we want to account for social values, for the intrinsic good of institutional, community, and associative activities, by a conception of justice that in its theoretical basis is individualistic.

John Rawls, *A Theory of Justice*

Guess what, people? Politics is about *what's in it for me*. Now, the socialist case is that what's good for everybody is best for everybody, and I think that that's a persuasive case. But there has to be an element of self-interest in it, too, to hook people who don't *already have your point of view*.

Matt Christman, *Chapo Trap House*, Episode 426

Introduction: What Is This Thing Called "Socialism"?

This book is meant for readers who are curious about socialism but are not ready to buy into it. To make the best case for socialism, the book addresses itself to readers who are pretty sure that they don't buy it.

This book is for *soloists*, that is, for people who are not drawn to the idea of leading their lives as if society were one big camping trip, where share-and-share-alike is the rule of the day. Soloists want to live their own lives, pursue their own dreams. Soloists are not solipsists: soloists realize that other people exist and have lives to live. Soloists are not loners any more than they are sociopaths. Soloists have loved ones and friends and associates: but they are not drawn to the idea of society itself as one big happy family. Family is small and intimate – society is huge and tends to be overwhelming.

Soloists are not egotists, either. They can enjoy competing and winning, but they don't live merely in order to dominate other people. Soloists are not put off by the idea that society itself is a kind of competition, with winners and losers. But soloists do insist that competition be fair, and that the rules be reasonable. They also insist that if society is to be run on a competitive basis, that losing should not mean being destroyed, and that the winners can't simply rig the rules so that no one else has a fair chance to win.

Some readers may already be drawn to socialism, or consider themselves to be socialists, and are impatient already. They may think that socialism begins with solidarity, whether with humanity as such or with fellow members of an oppressed social class. To these readers, pitching socialism to soloists is a misconceived, and probably doomed, endeavor. I recommend that these readers skip to the Afterword. Once having read the Afterword, they may wish to begin this book again, at the beginning.

So, what is *socialism*? In a socialist society, the means of production are public property. (What, precisely, the means of production consist of is addressed in Chapter 5.) Anybody who believes that society's key productive assets should work to benefit everyone should at least be curious about socialism. Strictly speaking, a socialist is somebody who believes that only a socialist society can be *just*. A society is just if its basic institutions are such that each individual member can expect to get his or her due. (You don't have to be a socialist to believe that.) A socialist is someone who denies that private ownership of the means of production is compatible, in the long run, with each of us getting what we are due.

Socialism should not be confused with (mere) progressivism. Progressives typically worry about extreme economic inequality and so they insist on taxing the wealthiest to subsidize the least-advantaged members of society. However, progressives typically do not *insist* on public ownership of the means of production. Their failure to do so is a big mistake, as I will show.

Socialism should not be confused with the welfare state. The welfare state serves to support those who cannot live decently upon the income they derive from their labor or the capital they own. Socialism is concerned with the specific problem of justice among producers. A welfare state can be tacked onto a capitalist society, in which the means of production are privately owned and the market solves the problem of giving each producer her due.

Socialists are strongly in favor of having a welfare state; but a welfare state does not amount to socialism. In fact, the first welfare state was instituted in Germany by Otto von Bismarck, who was no enemy of private ownership of the means of production. Experience shows that in capitalist countries the welfare state is constantly opposed by ideologies that demand privatization, austerity, and "personal responsibility." The welfare state in social democracies is exposed to the same pressures. The welfare state is more secure in socialist societies, owing in part to the stronger sense of solidarity among citizens who share ownership of the means of production.

There is more to justice than public ownership of the means of production. Justice requires democracy – the rule of the many – rather than an autocracy or an oligopoly – the rule of one or the few. In a just society every adult has certain political rights, including the right to vote, the right to put questions on the voting agenda, and the right to run for public office. Justice requires *democratic* socialism. Saying so is no argument: that comes in the chapters ahead. But I want to be clear that the socialism advocated here is democratic socialism, not a socialist society run by one party, or by one class of society. I won't keep repeating "democratic socialism," because that is what I mean from here on out by the word "socialism."

Justice requires that each person be recognized as having certain basic rights, such as the right to free speech, free exercise of religion, choice of occupation, bodily integrity, privacy, and so on. Respecting these basic rights means that laws cannot justly infringe them. What if the law is backed by the majority, and enacted democratically? The democratic socialism advocated in this book is *liberal*, meaning that these basic rights are immune from legal infringement, even if the majority wants them to be infringed. To spell it all out, the subject of the book is *liberal democratic socialism*. But, again, I will refer to it simply as socialism.

The thesis of the book is simply this: justice requires

socialism. You, the reader, are entitled to ask *why*? What is the argument?

The argument is two-part. The first part is about justice, and it shows that – despite our differences – we can all agree to certain principles of justice. The central principles that emerge are these:

> *Principle of Political Equality*: Citizens who are equally able and equally motivated should have an equal chance to influence political decisions, regardless of wealth and income.

> *Principle of Reciprocity*: Economic inequality is allowed so long as it can be seen to benefit all representative social classes.

The argument for these principles is a development of the social contract tradition within political philosophy. It is important to distinguish three different roles a social contract story could play.

The first is as historical explanation. Political societies, or some of them, might have come into existence in virtue of a social compact. Some of their present characteristics might be understood in terms of how they arose. These characteristics could include normative ones, like legitimacy. We could term this the genealogical role.

The second role is as a recipe by which we might go about founding a political society. This could be useful to know even if no actual polity has ever arisen this way. The recipe could be written in a way that assures that the polity has legitimate authority over its members. The recipe could also tell us how to reconstitute a polity, so that it would acquire a legitimacy it theretofore had lacked. We could term this the prescriptive role.

The third role a social contract theory could play would be to formulate a critical standard by which, or a critical standpoint from which, to assess existing and possible institutions. We might have a better appreciation of the status quo if we could explain it in terms that show that it is just, or nearly so, or tending toward justice, with reference to principles that could or should command rational assent. We can term this the critical role.

If a social contract story plays its critical role well, it might reconcile us to the society we currently inhabit. It could do this even if the theory failed as a genealogical explanation of our society, and even if there were no real possibility of it serving as a prescription for getting actual, unanimous, agreement among all the many members of our society. The critical role might be convincingly performed even if no actual agreement ever occurred and were never realistically possible for any developed nation.

The social contract idea used here is meant to play the critical role, and to be consistent with the form in which it was reanimated in the latter half of the twentieth century by philosopher John Rawls. No prior acquaintance with Rawls is assumed. Readers who are already familiar with Rawls's theory could proceed directly to Part Two.

The second part of the book applies the principles of justice derived in Part One to our present-day circumstances. The same method of argument used in Part One is followed, but with attention given to the fact that we live today with the consequences of the Industrial Revolution. Socialism emerges as the only type of regime that can be counted on to realize the two principles derived in Part One.

A short concluding section summarizes the argument. An Afterword addresses some questions that already committed socialists may have. Newly committed socialists might want to ask them, too.

Part One
Getting to Principles of Justice

1

The Social Contract

Life in a society is like a game, in some ways. In other ways, not. Both games and social life itself involve rules. In both cases, the rules leave it up to each of us to make a wide range of choices for ourselves. At the same time, in both cases, the rules disallow certain kinds of choices. In both cases, rules help us to know what to expect and how to plan what to do. Rules have this advantage only if they are normally obeyed by all concerned.

Every rule that is normally followed within a group of people has at least this one virtue, that of predictability. Predictability may mean little to those of us soloists who value authenticity and free spontaneity. Yet even we who highly value spontaneity can appreciate rules that allow us to do as we please while confident that we may do so without interference from others.

There are differences between games and social life itself. Games depend on rules to make them what they are. Playing a game is more than simply being at play. Social life, by contrast, conceivably could exist in the absence of rules. True, it is not easy to imagine a society of people thriving in the utter absence of rules; and, true also, social rules of many sorts surround us in the actual conditions of modern life.

If we are suspicious of the contrast, we might say that human interaction is always and everywhere subject to at least one permissive rule: such as, you may do as you think necessary in order to survive. So, where there's life, there is at least one rule in play. It is harder to picture a game that consists of a single permissive rule, such as, you may do as you think it fun to do. Following that rule merely means being at play.

Another difference is a difference in the stakes. Not all games are competitive, and among the many competitive games, the stakes are typically kept low. Losing a game does not cost one one's life (notwithstanding the ball games of the Aztecs). Competition for the necessities of life can be different. In a world in which these necessities (food, drink, shelter, clothing, etc.) are scarce, losing out can mean starvation or death by thirst or exposure.

The major difference between games and society is this, though: we can choose which games to enter into, once we are adults. If we dislike poker we can play parcheesi, and if we don't like either, or don't like to play games, we can choose not to play at all. Social life and social rules are different. We are required to play by these rules, like it or not. We have no real choice. Even if we had the means, if we pulled up our tent-stakes and moved out of the country, we would only land ourselves amidst another society and its rules.

Here is a thought. Suppose we know that we will have to play a game, and that the stakes will be very high. The purpose of the game will be to produce and re-produce the conditions needed to do other things, pursue other goals, of whatever kind. Once the game is under way, each player will have two roles. One role will be to engage in production. The other role will be to do other things, perhaps to play other games, sports, or to pursue other leisure activities, to socialize, read, watch videos, meditate, whatever.

We don't want to exaggerate the distinction between the two roles. Producing the things we do can be what we most want to do. Or it can be merely what we do to make a living. One thing, though, is hard to exaggerate: that is, the degree to which our freedom to pursue the ends we set for ourselves is dependent on the cooperation of everyone else, or at least on their not interfering. So also, it is hard to exaggerate the degree to which the things we do merely to make a living depend upon other people valuing what we do and make, and being ready to exchange things we want and need for the things we do and make.

So, to continue the thought: suppose we have no real choice but to play a high-stakes game, but at the same time we do have a say in making up the rules that will determine how the game will be played. What rules, if any, would we agree to?

This is a big question. We might approach it by first asking, what *kind* of rules would we be willing to consider? The answer to this question will depend on what we want the rules to accomplish. All rules – other than the permissive rule, "Anything goes" – are constraining. As soloists, we chafe at constraint and love liberty. Why would we ever submit to any constraining rules?

The obvious and familiar answer to that question is that if anything goes, no one will be secure. Everyone will then be less free. That is bad enough, and if people feel insecure, they will invest their time and energy in ways that are wasteful and unproductive. Rules against using force against others, and against defrauding others, are needed, at the very least. Otherwise, people will be too distrustful and too insecure to expend their energies and wits on things like cultivating crops and improving land, building roads and making tools as well as weapons.

At this point, many will insist that we distinguish between two kinds of rules. One kind of rule could be called natural rules, or laws of nature. God-given rules could be counted under this heading. Thou shalt not steal, thou shalt not kill, thou shalt not bear false witness, and so forth. The other kind of rules are artificial rules, made up by people. The laws of nature just listed are constraining rules. If they are followed, there need be no insecurity. There could be agriculture, and artisanship, and manufacture, and trade, and prosperity. If only people would harken to the law of nature. Human-made laws would be unnecessary. Or, where they were necessary, they could be derived by applying some more general law of nature.

The natural law need not be thought of in terms of divine commands. They might simply belong to the natural order of the universe. Or, it could be that humans simply evolved in a way that disposes normal individuals to acknowledge and abide by certain natural rules, which we can refer to collectively as the natural law.

The idea of having a conscience meshes well with the idea of natural rules. God might implant these rules in our hearts. Reason might reveal them to our minds. Evolution might have selected groups that feature a heritable disposition to observe them. By whichever route they were bequeathed to us, why would they not be enough for the purpose of security and prosperity? And, as if by design, they would determine the standard of what is just. Justice is conformity with the rules of natural law.

The problem with this is that we seem fated to disagree in fundamental ways about the content of the natural law. Even where we think we are close to consensus about some of its content, we disagree about how that content applies. Think of the Old Testament commandment, "Thou shalt not kill." Does this forbid killing in self-defense, or not? Does it forbid killing non-human animals, or not? Does it forbid killing fetuses, or not? People have very strongly held but mutually irreconcilable views about each of these questions.

Suppose we are among those who agree that killing in self-defense is not unjust. We all assent to the proposition that a person attacked by another is permitted to defend herself, even with deadly force, if deadly force is necessary to avoid a deadly attack. What if she is mistaken about the need to use force, should she be punished? Should she have to retreat before resorting to deadly force? Or may she stand her ground? Should she have to retreat from

her home before resorting to deadly force? It is unlikely
that we who agree that self-defensive force is sometimes
justifiable will ever agree unanimously as to each of these
subsidiary questions.

Set aside the issue whether there are any correct answers
to these questions. There may be, there might not be.
But if we cannot agree about what those answers are,
the answers cannot well serve to promote our security
and prosperity. If the only rules we live by are the law of
nature, we are liable to be sucked into endless, irresolvable
controversy unless we have a way of dealing with our deep
disagreements about questions like this.

Some of us would be satisfied to leave it to God or destiny
to deal with injustice. Leaving these matters unsettled is
unsatisfactory insofar as planning and effort depend
upon some degree of stability and security. Human life
cannot prosper, it seems, without some earthly, temporal
authority empowered to settle disruptive disputes and,
in doing so, to interpret the rules of justice. Further than
that, prosperity seems to require that some temporal
authority have the power to introduce new rules when
emergencies or changed circumstances demand them. This
would entail having power to limit or even to extinguish
older, established rules, when they had outlived their
rationale.

A soloist will not readily concede her natural liberty
to do as she pleases while leaving others equally free. A
soloist, however, can see the advantage of having certain
rules artificially laid down to regulate social interactions.
Rules of the road, for example. There is no natural law
that dictates that vehicular traffic should stay to the left
side or to the right side of the road. It is not even obvious
that there is a natural law requiring that traffic stay to one
side or another – if vehicular traffic were kept as slow as
pedestrian traffic, then this sort of stick-to-one-side rule
would no more be needed than a rule mandating that
pedestrians stay on one particular side of the sidewalk.
But where vehicular traffic picks up speed, even the most

determined soloist can see the huge advantage of having an artificial rule.

Not so fast ... Artificial rules can bind a soloist only insofar as she, the individual, *consents* to them. Or so she maintains: that's one of the things that makes her a soloist. She is not alone in believing this: in fact, the mainstream tradition in English-speaking countries holds that government can only be legitimated by the consent of the governed. Without the consent of the governed, there is no basic difference between a government and a protection racket. Ever since the divine-right-of-kings theory went out of fashion a few centuries ago, every modern nation-state at least *claims* to rule by and with the consent of the people.

This idea of government by consent has to be examined with care, lest it be misunderstood. No government claims to give each citizen a veto over laws she disagrees with. Government by consent does not mean, and has never meant, government by consensus as to each law and every application of a law. Consensus, that is, universal agreement, does have a place however.

The idea is that consensus – universal assent – is necessary at the highest level, but only at that level. As to lesser matters, the majority may decide. In other words, soloists (and all others) shall agree, unanimously, to a basic charter that outlines the conditions under which a majority decision will be decisive and binding upon all (including the minority who disagree with a subsidiary decision, law, or rule). This basic charter is what is meant by the phrase, "the social contract."

For government by consent to be effective, the rules cannot be subject to veto, exception, or override at the whim of anyone who happens to feel they are misguided, or finds them inconvenient. On the other hand, for government by consent to mean anything, there has to be unanimous consent at some level. That level is the level at which there is a basic charter that accomplishes two things. First, there has to be an agreement as to the overall type of lawmaking process. Second, there has to be an agreement setting a limit to what matters are proper subjects of the lawmaking process – or an agreement *not* to set any limit.

Lawmaking processes can take a variety of forms. Unanimity is unnecessary to each detail (e.g., at-large versus single-member districts in a legislature); nevertheless, unanimity is needed as to certain key characteristics of government. Soloists think of themselves as free beings. Soloists recognize no authority but that of free reason itself. Soloists reject dictatorship as a legitimate lawmaking process. But why? Why would a soloist reject lawmaking by herself as dictator? The answer is simple. Soloists are not solipsists. Soloists recognize the existence of others, and their possession of the power freely to reason. Soloists recognize others as free equals.

Not as equals in every respect, of course. Others will differ in age, size, strength, looks, intelligence, tastes, experience, patience, sensitivity, ability to distinguish sounds and colors, and myriad other ways. The capacity possessed equally by all who accept the basic charter is the capacity to understand it and to be guided by it. Agreement to the charter cannot be binding except as to those who can understand it and can abide by it.

Soloists, then, recognize the pressing need for social rules and a common power to enforce them. Soloists recognize that there is a variety of conflicting ideas about what the natural rules are and what any artificial rules should be. Soloists accept that there is a pressing need for an agreed process to settle important disputes and to make rules to enable everyone to feel secure and to plan out their lives. Soloists accept that government cannot be a matter of unanimous agreement "all the way down" to the smallest detail. Soloists do not aspire to dictate to others; yet, at the same time, they are unready to be dictated to, even by the majority.

Soloists will therefore insist on two things. First, that some things are simply not on the table for majority decision. One's inner life, one's beliefs, to begin with, are never to be dictated by others. Society may try to persuade, but the individual's right to dissent, in thought and speech, is sacred to soloists. Second, even within the sphere of matters that society might legitimately regulate, the individual must always have an equal say in determining whether to regulate, and how.

Another way of putting this is to say that a soloist will accept no government as legitimate unless it is both *liberal* and *democratic*. By "liberal," I only mean that a liberal society is one that respects the individual as the final authority over matters of conscience, speech, and final ends. By "democratic," I mean that a society's political power is shared among all citizens in equal measure. In other words, citizens interested to the same degree in some political issue, and possessing the same articulate grasp of it, ought to have the same influence over its outcome – regardless of their relative social or economic advantages.

The social contract limits the legitimate scope of government. To accomplish this, the scope of the social contract must be wider than that of government. The social contract applies to the basic structure of society but not to every relationship or institution within society. The social contract consists of principles that fix the standard of justice that basic institutions must meet; but they do not apply to the inner workings of, say, the family, or friendships, or churches, unions, clubs, or business associations. A church or a social club may have any sort of internal government it chooses, but it must obey rules of general applicability, and it cannot enforce its internal rules by imprisoning or executing disobedient members.

The idea of the basic structure is vague. It derives from a more basic idea, that of society itself conceived as a fair system of cooperation for mutual benefit. The social contract is meant to set out the rules soloists would accept as defining the social game, whose goal is to produce the goods needed by all. The basic structure consists of the political and economic institutions that are the manifestation of this common productive enterprise.

It is as though society was setting itself up as a business which people had no choice but to work for. The question for soloists is: what kind of rules should constitute such an enterprise? That is, what rules (if any) would I, as a soloist, accept as having my assent – even though I was never asked beforehand to accept them?

The social contract, then, applies to more than just the form and limits of the government. It also applies to the major institutions of the economy, such as the forms of property that are recognized and protected by the common, public power. At first glance, someone might think that was entirely a matter of natural law, and that the proper role of government can only be to protect private holdings, the right to which precedes any public power. This unfocused first appearance is illusory. Property and ownership mean nothing in the absence of a common power to define and enforce them. Even if they did mean something in a state of mere nature, they would be insecure due to the fact that people reasonably disagree about what gives anyone a right to exclude others from using and enjoying the earth and its fruits, which were – some say – originally given by God to humanity in common.

Surely, even in a state of nature, an individual right to use and enjoy a thing – a right exclusive of the rights of all others – has to have arisen at some point. Even if you had as much right as I to pick a low-hanging fruit from the branch of a tree, unless you are starving you have no right to snatch it out of my hand as I bite into it. Surely also, even if you had as much right as I did to enclose a plot of ground and cultivate it, if in fact I was the first, and raised a crop, I am entitled to that crop to the exclusion of any claim you might make.

It would be unreasonable to deny that the first-comer has some kind of claim to the fruit, and the laborer to the crop. This does not take us very far, though. When we try to generalize the idea of acquiring a natural title to stuff by mixing our labor with it, we don't get much further. Let's assume we own our bodies and we are to be credited for the good we voluntarily do by moving our bodies. That cannot mean that we have a claim to own every thing we mix our labor with, even if we mix it with the intention of making that thing our exclusive property. As philosopher Robert Nozick put it, if you take your can of tomato juice – which is incontestably yours, let's say – and mix it with the ocean, what reason is there to think you gain an ocean by that act, rather than lose your tomato juice?

We should pause to take stock and to appreciate the fact that, despite areas of disagreement and uncertainty, we do agree that – prior to institutions and enforcement and a social contract – there are certain ownership claims that are beyond serious dispute. No soloist will agree to a social contract that does not guarantee her absolute right to her body. A soloist might consider donating a kidney, but she would never consent to a social contract that, in principle, left open the possibility that her kidney might be taken from her against her will.

A soloist can imagine circumstances in which the greater good might be served by transplanting one of her kidneys into the body of a needy and worthy hospital patient. It might be that the needy patient is an eminent virologist, who is on the verge of a discovery that will save millions of lives. It might be that the soloist and the virologist share a rare blood type, such that only her kidney will do. Even so, a soloist could reasonably refuse to sign onto a social contract that, in principle, did not respect her basic right to bodily integrity. She will not agree to any contract that makes her right to her body conditional upon "the calculus of social interests," she might say.

Likewise, a soloist can reasonably reject principles that allow the calculus of social interests, as decided by a majority or even by the unanimous opinion of others, to dictate what she is allowed to think. Again, this is not because the soloist cannot imagine circumstances in which it would be better for everyone if, for solidarity's sake, everyone was required to adopt a single form of worship or profession of philosophical belief. She can. But she holds that her conscience is a pearl beyond price. Even if she could change her beliefs, nothing in the world would induce her to allow society to dictate what they are.

Whoa. I'm making some pretty sweeping generalizations about soloists. Some of us soloists might not value our bodily integrity more highly than the lives of millions. We might know we are too squeamish to donate a kidney even if we happened to know that, in the circumstances, millions of lives would be saved as a result. We might agree to be forced to do something we knew we could not bring ourselves to do without being forced.

Likewise, some of us soloists know that we might be profoundly mistaken about fundamental matters, and so we might not object to being forced – if it would make things better – to worship in a certain way or to mouth certain opinions, pledge certain allegiances, and so on. We might even agree that it could be better if we actually came to believe certain things that we could never have believed without having been indoctrinated – brainwashed, browbeaten – into believing them.

It is starting to seem as though there are no limits to what a soloist will agree to, if the alternative to agreement is sufficiently dire. If a soloist believes, with Thomas Hobbes, that without everyone's surrendering to an absolute sovereign, life would be "solitary, poore, nasty, brutish, and short," then the social contract is a *carte blanche*, upon which the sovereign power may scribble, erase, and re-scribble whatever it thinks best.

Pursuing the idea of a social contract looks now as if it leads to a dilemma. Soloists either remain true to themselves, and reserve the right to live by their own judgments regardless of what the rules of the contract say, or they surrender everything to a common power, which dictates terms it then enforces, "with the sword," as Hobbes liked to say. There's no contract in the first alternative. And, despite appearances, there's no real contract in the second either: only a blank check.

The key to avoiding the dilemma lies in the possibility

of arriving at a social contract that soloists are sure can be kept because the parties could rationally choose to keep it, without being forced. Soloists know that it takes all kinds to make a society, both soloist kinds and non-soloist kinds. Soloists also know that there are certain terms to which they might verbally agree, but which they could not keep, if it came to it. Therefore, soloists also know there are terms that others could not keep, even if, for the sake of peace, they gave their sincere, solemn word that they would. The task, then, is to find a set of principles to govern the basic structure of society – society conceived as a fair, productive cooperative venture – that all parties could reasonably expect to keep and to be kept by all others as well.

Soloists are not suckers. They know the difference between people who are committed to keeping their word and can be trusted to do so, and other people who cannot. Soloists know that there is a further difference that is equally significant. There are people who overestimate their ability to keep their word. Any pact or contract will impose burdens on the parties. Some parties are sincere in their commitment to the terms of a pact, and the terms are within their power to keep even when the burdens of doing so are great. Some parties are not sincere in their commitment, and will do as they please whenever they figure it benefits them to do so. These insincere people can be expected to give lip-service to a social contract merely in order to reap the benefit of the trust that others extend to them. And then there are people who sincerely mean to keep their bargains but, when push comes to shove, lack the fortitude to keep them.

Many socialists, it is sad to say, fall into this third group. They sincerely mean to let solidarity and sympathy motivate them to keep a social contract that requires sharing the burdens of social existence equally. But when they see the chance of gaining an advantage for themselves they find it too good to pass up. This is especially likely to happen if the special advantage is one that benefits their offspring or close family.

Think of people who, though vocal supporters of public education, send their own children to expensive private schools. Hypocrisy is a sign that someone has underestimated what we can call the "strains of commitment." What distinguishes the hypocrite, who cannot practice what she preaches, from a mere charlatan, is that the hypocrite is sincere in her preachments while the charlatan is not. Soloists have to be wary of both. A soloist has no interest in signing onto high-sounding proclamations that cannot withstand these strains.

A social contract that cannot withstand the strains of commitment fails to satisfy the need that makes a contract desirable. Parties need mutual assurance that their interactions will be peaceful and predictable, and this assurance is missing in a state of mere nature. It is a fact of human nature that self-interest is a powerful motive; but so also is the desire to punish, even when punishing is costly. The perception that another is taking unfair advantage in a transaction is often enough to cause a person to forego a benefit. A social contract will likely fail unless it is seen by all as *fair*. A fair contract is likelier (though never certain) to supply the need for mutual assurance among the parties that all are willing and able to uphold their end of the bargain. What has been called the "assurance problem" is the problem that people are unwilling to "go first" in limiting their liberty, unless they have some assurance that others will not take unfair advantage.

The assurance problem has to make soloists wary of entering into any social contract. Let's explore the possibility of adjusting the terms of the contract to increase the likelihood that it will be perceived as fair. A sense of fairness can be counted upon to reinforce trust. If both self-interest and fairness are recruited in support of a compact, it will be more stable than if it is supported only by the one or the other. Moreover, a sense of solidarity can arise among a group of strangers over the course of interactions perceived as fair and mutually beneficial. Where the members of a group adhere to a set of common principles, and know that they all do so adhere, then we can say that they share a sense of justice.

The question thus resolves into this: If we think of society in the way suggested, as a fair cooperative scheme for mutual benefit, are there any principles that it would be unreasonable to reject, given that, without a shared sense of justice informed by some such principles, everyone in society would be much, much worse off?

It is hard to assess how useful the idea of a social contract is without knowing the principles it might contain. Here is a way we might identify such principles. Imagine we, as soloists, know we are going to be forced to play a special type of game. The purpose of the game is to provide what people generally need in order to live and to thrive. By "in order to thrive," I mean in order to pursue whatever personal goals they choose to set for themselves, whatever those goals happen to be. These goods will be in drastically shorter supply if players cannot agree upon a general set of rules to assure the background conditions needed for social life to go on.

A soloist can begin to identify the desired principles by conducting a thought-experiment, beginning with tentative rules designed to optimize her own chances of success in pursuit of her own goals. The soloist then asks whether she could count on other soloists to agree to these rules. If the answer is No, they could not be trusted, then the tentative rule goes into the waste basket. If the answer is Yes, then the rule passes the test, and becomes part of a social contract that *could* be agreed to by reasonable soloists.

It is already obvious anyway, but it is worth noting the difference between a contract that *could* be agreed to, and a contract that *would* be agreed to. It is plausible to say that if social existence in modern conditions requires that there be some social contract, then a contract that all reasonable people could assent to is one that no reasonable person would refuse to agree to.

It has also got to be acknowledged that there is a

profound difference between a contract that *has been* agreed to and one that *would be* agreed to. There is a binding force an actual agreement possesses that a hypothetical agreement lacks. It is important not to exaggerate this point. It does not imply that a hypothetical agreement has no force whatever. When cooperation is necessary to benefit everyone, as when a disaster otherwise impends, it is sometimes permissible to force people to cooperate, if the terms are fair ones. If a group of strangers is suddenly cast onto the ocean in an overloaded boat, it is not unfair if everyone is required to stay put, lest the boat capsize.

The analogy to the conditions of life generally is imperfect, of course. The point here is merely that it will be interesting to know if the thought-experiment turns up plausible candidate principles to serve as the content of a hypothetical contract. If it does, we might then pursue the question of what provision those principles make for the treatment of people who refuse to accept or abide by the social contract. Until we have an at least initially plausible set of principles in hand, the question would be premature.

I have already said that a soloist would not accept any form of government that was not *liberal* (in the sense defined) and *democratic*. The reason is not so much that she values liberty and autonomy more highly than peace, as it is that she recognizes that there are others who – though desirous of peace – do not value it above liberty and autonomy. Whatever her own order of values, she recognizes that a social contract cannot promote peace unless it can be embraced by people who do not share all of her values and her priorities.

A soloist is unlikely to need to be persuaded that the constitution of a just society has to respect certain fundamental rights and liberties. These must be equal for all parties to the basic compact, and for two reasons. Equal liberty is an attractive ideal, for one thing. For another, a set of principles that did not guarantee equal liberty would not be stable. Those who perceived (correctly or otherwise) that their place in society was one of lesser liberty could not be trusted to accept the basic structure.

Or could they? Here, we have to make distinctions between different kinds of goods. We consider society as a cooperative venture whose aim is to produce the instrumental goods needed as the means for free citizens to pursue whatever private ends they might choose to set for themselves. What goes into this category is a variety of things: liberties of all sorts, occupational opportunities, educational opportunities, political power, income, and wealth. Let's call this category the category of primary goods, adopting the terminology of John Rawls. The question needing our attention at this point is whether a soloist, designing rules, would treat all of these primary goods as more-or-less fungible, and thus as admitting of substitutions. Or would she assign certain goods to a higher category, such that she would reject any suggestion to accept a lesser amount of them in return for a greater amount of goods from a lower category?

We have already taken the point that a soloist knows that some members of society hold that certain primary goods are priceless. Persons of faith would not trade the right to practice according to the rituals of their particular faith for any amount of money. Christians take the lesson of the last temptation of Christ: Satan promised Jesus all worldly goods, if he would foreswear his faith. Christ would not and Christians would not. The soloist need not be a Christian herself to realize that she cannot expect those who are Christian to accept a social contract that would even consider the advantages of imposing a uniform worship on all citizens.

Another way of putting the point is this: if a non-believing soloist set aside the knowledge that she is a non-believer, she would reject a social contract that treated all primary goods as interchangeable. She would have to take seriously the possibility that she herself was, or was to become, a person of faith. What she would not risk for herself, from this perspective, is what it would be unreasonable to ask others to risk. A social contract cannot succeed if it makes demands that cannot be met even by those who sincerely promise to meet them.

The significance of this is to reinforce the point that a soloist has reason to reject any but a "liberal" social contract, which gives prior protection to certain basic rights and liberties, such as the freedoms of speech, expression, worship, and conscience. "Prior protection" means that society rejects out of hand the temptation to explore the possibility of increasing the supply of other primary goods, such as wealth or educational opportunity, by imposing an orthodox faith.

The soloist can acknowledge that it is possible that a religiously homogeneous society might become a wealthier society. An established religion might possibly be better able to instill an entrepreneurial ethic, or to remove controversy, once the steps needed to impose uniformity had been taken. A liberal society will not merely question the factual basis for such thinking: it will reject it even if there are reasons to be weighed in its favor.

The group of basic rights guaranteed in a liberal democracy has, at its core, the right of freedom of thought and speech. Historically, the idea of a social contract both lent support to and drew support from the conviction that matters of personal faith and profession ought not to be controverted in the give-and-take of ordinary politics. Controverting deeply divisive matters of faith in the forum of ordinary politics has proven to incline to violence. The horrors and devastation of the Wars of Religion of the sixteenth and seventeenth centuries, in Britain and Europe, impressed this lesson on the minds of thinkers of the time and ever since.

Even in that era, it was possible to retain the conviction that one's own faith is the true faith while conceding that it was a bad idea to try to use political power to force non-believers to share one's faith. This meant that the legitimacy of government could rest on something other than an appeal to religious truth or to divine authority.

Civil peace *had* to rest on an ideological foundation that
could be agreed to by practitioners of different faiths. So,
the idea of a social contract and the idea of toleration
were mutually supporting. Soloists of all nations can
reason together, and with non-soloists, confident that
any acceptable social contract will respect freedom of
individual conscience, and the further freedoms that give
it meaning, such as speech and association.

But what else? The strains of commitment are most
manageable in the context of widespread (though not
necessarily universal) agreement that a certain matter is
"off the table," so to speak. You may know someone who
believes it is his life's mission to save souls by converting
them to the one true faith. Such a believer may have
trouble accepting secularization of the public schools,
where attendance at tender ages is mandatory. It goes
against the urgings of his faith for him not to promote
it anywhere and any way he can, so his commitment to
a liberal charter of government is a strain for him. He is
better able to manage this strain because he knows that
you and I, too, are not allowed to try to program the
elementary curriculum to promote our faiths, which could
be quite different from his. It is easier to manage the strain
because we know, and know that each other know, that
it is fair that we all accept liberty of conscience and what
it entails.

Now, he – the believer I just described – might disagree
that you and I honor the pact between us all if, say,
voluntary prayer is excluded from the school day in public
elementary schools. He might say that excluding prayer
in effect dictates non-prayer, which is a rite peculiar to a
secularized religion that he can reasonably reject. Does he
have a point? If he does, prospects of any secure advance
beyond the open religious warfare of centuries past look
dim. We all would seem to remain in what Hobbes called
"the precincts of battalle," simply biding our time until the
balance of forces favors our particular side.

This is a serious question. It would be too quick to brush

it aside as merely a sophistical confusion between keeping religion in brackets and imposing a secular "religion." Soloists (and others) can get a clearer picture of the issue by trying to imagine what rule they could accept if they did not know their religious faith and whether they had one at all. (This is a method we've already used, to test whether others can fairly be asked to agree to a certain claim: would we be making it if we were standing in their shoes?) The fact is that most people have come to accept a principle of religious toleration even though it is also true that they have various, and even mutually incompatible, reasons for accepting it.

Some accept religious toleration because they are not religious. Some accept religious toleration because their religion teaches it as an article of their faith. Some accept religious toleration because their religion allows it and it seems a good idea besides. Most people belong to one or another of these groups. None of them need to subscribe to the proposition that all religions should be tolerated because they are all harmless fantasies. We can hope for an "overlapping consensus" supporting the principle of liberty of conscience. We can hope for this because we can see that such a consensus does not depend upon any wider agreement on the truth or content of religious doctrines.

We discover that we can agree on at least this term of a social contract even though we disagree about many other things. The social contract, seen in this light, becomes even more appealing to soloists because it shows how we might manage to navigate a social world that is radically pluralistic – meaning, a society that contains a huge and even increasing variety of beliefs, hopes, interests, and projects. So long as the social contract allows people sufficient space to work out their lives for themselves, it liberates us far more than it constrains us, despite the fact that it does indeed constrain us.

From this point forward, I will assume that we soloists are confident that all reasonable people can agree to a principle that gives everyone, equally, a special protection in matters of private conscience. This leaves open myriad questions of application and detail, and we will need to agree on some procedure for resolving those – but this does not in itself undercut the foundation we have begun. We don't have to resort to argument over the meaning of life and the place of humans in the cosmic scheme in order to work to extend the idea of a social contract. We share a "public political culture" containing ideas we all understand and accept. Liberty of conscience is one of them. We are all "on the same page" as to this shared and durable "fixed point" against which to compare other matters.

What other terms can we add, applying the same method we have used before? What other terms would we want included, if we did not know what our own position in society, and our own particular strengths and weaknesses, happen to be? In other words, what kind of society would we want to be born into, not knowing which of the people in it we would be?

2
Why Economic Inequality?

If we conceive of society itself as a cooperative scheme for mutual benefit, how are the goods it makes possible to be divided?

If your first thought was to say, "Equally!" you would not be alone. Even philosopher Robert Nozick, that celebrated soloist, might chime in too, if the goods concerned had fallen into our laps like manna from heaven. But, as Nozick was quick to point out, the goods we are concerned with are not manna from heaven. They are the product of human effort, individual effort, in the last analysis. Even the products of cooperative effort are, from a soloist's viewpoint, the product of a combination of individual contributions. Individual efforts typically vary. One worker is stronger, another smarter. The smart worker typically does smart work, but is not perfect. Not all contributions are equal.

So, from Nozick's point of view, were we to adopt a distributive principle as part of a social contract, it should not be one of equal distribution. Nor should it be the one Marx and Engels projected for a fully communist society, "from each according to his ability, to each according to his need." From a soloist/libertarian perspective (which the later Nozick confessed misgivings about) a principle of just distribution had better be something like, "to each according to his perceived contribution to society," as judged by, well ... by what he was able to earn in the labor market.

It is widely assumed that a principle of equality will govern in a socialist society. And, it is true that equality has a role to play in a socialist account of distributive justice. Even so, the principle announced by Marx and Engels was not egalitarian. The more able contribute more than the less able, and people are not assumed to be equally able. The needier receive more than the less needy, and people are needy in different degrees. Marx and Engels count as socialists, but they were not egalitarians, full stop. Lenin, who was a socialist (if not a liberal democratic one), was fond of repeating St. Paul's dictum, "Who does not work, shall not eat." The Bolshevik Revolution was motivated, in large part, by a sense of outrage at a social structure in which those who worked hardest got the least in return.

Socialism, then, cannot be reduced to simple egalitarianism, nor can it be equated with an attitude of share-and-share-alike. It is true that the Marxian critique of the wage relation under capitalism has had a profound influence. On the other hand, socialists agree that diligent effort that benefits others in society ought to be rewarded. Moreover, many today are persuaded that socialism is not incompatible with letting individual incomes from work be determined by market mechanisms. Socialism, recall, is in its essence the tenet that the means of production ought to be, and to always remain, the people's joint property. (If this tenet seems to you to be a matter of dispute among socialists, think of it as my stipulation.) How these means of production are to be deployed is for democratic decision, not for decision by private owners. To say this is not yet to say how incomes are determined.

A socialist society might choose to provide access to the means of production at no charge to those needing to use them. It might choose to lease them, and retain the rents for reinvestment. It might choose to distribute rents as dividends, equally, to all, or to dedicate rents to providing public goods of various kinds. All of these are options in a socialist society. What is not an option is for private owners to garner rents from those needing access to the means of production. That is the essence of capitalism, and it is unjust. That's the conclusion toward which this book argues. That private ownership of society's means of production is unjust can be seen as we pursue the question, what principle of distributive justice would soloists include in their social contract?

A just society is one in which each person gets what she is due. All can agree to this. Disagreement begins the moment we raise the obvious next question, how can we tell what is due to a person, each person? The idea that there is some objective, external metric that could be applied to make this determination, continuously, for everyone, seems hopeless. So also is the idea that there is some set of facts about a person which, if fed into an algorithm of some kind, could be converted into a precise figure stating the income and wealth that person is due. That seems equally hopeless.

A much more appealing way of thinking about the problem of distributive justice is to think of a productive society as being, in a way, like a fair competition. We set up a competitive game in a way such that, if the rules are followed, then the final score is what it ought to be, whatever it happens to be. If we agree to play a game by a set of rules, and the rules are followed, then the outcome is fair, whatever it happens to be. There is no external standard that the outcome has to be checked against.

Roulette and other games of chance are like this. (They are not like, say, a game of guess-your-weight.) An analogy suggests itself. If the basic institutions of society are set up fairly, and the rules we agree to are followed, then the package of basic goods delivered to each simply *is* what each is due, whatever it happens to contain in the form of individual wealth and income.

This takes us back to the question posed in the previous chapter: what rules would we agree to, if we were forced to play a game upon which our lives and livelihoods depended? If the rules are fair, and adhered to, then there should be no further question about the justice of distributions of goods to individual players. A tennis player who loses a match by a score of 6–0, 4–6, 4–6 cannot complain that the prize was due to her and not her opponent. The loser won more points, but the rules of tennis specify that the winner is the contestant who is the first to win two (or three) sets. If she objects to that method of scoring, she is not pressing a claim of injustice. If she doesn't like the way the rules of tennis are written, and can do nothing to get them changed, she should consider taking up another sport.

The analogy suggested here would be faulty if it distracted us from the fact that different sets of rules can make for better and worse games. Some games are no fun at all. Like "Fifty-two Pickup," in which an older sibling throws a deck of cards on the floor for the younger to pick up. Some games run according to rules that give a small but significant advantage to one of the players (the casino, or "house"). Many people find casino games fun to play, even though they know that, statistically, they are bound to be net losers over the long run. People who play casino games compulsively, or risk ruin by staking all, are to be pitied.

Some games have flaws in their design that may not be obvious. The board game Monopoly is like this. Whoever controls the orange-colored properties – New York Avenue, Tennessee Avenue, St. James Place – will usually win. This is because those properties lie six, eight, and nine places after the Jail. Any player who lands on the "Go to Jail" square or draws a "Go to Jail" card has to take another run past the orange properties. It isn't obvious at first, but overall, the chances of landing on an orange property are greater than the chances of landing on a property of any other type. Once someone has a monopoly of orange properties, in all probability the other players will slowly, slowly be ground into bankruptcy. If two players each own an orange property, and each is wise to the decisive advantage of an orange monopoly, both will hold out, and the game can go on forever (or seem to).

The inventor of the original Monopoly game, Elizabeth Magie, intended it to discredit, rather than to celebrate, the political economy of her time, the first so-called Gilded Age (ours being the second). She called it "The Landlord's Game." The Landlord's Game came with two alternative sets of rules. One set of rules was meant to reward players for benefitting all. The other set of rules rewarded the player who bled the others dry. Only the second set of rules made it into the commercialized game of Monopoly.

In the real world, no adult is forced to play Monopoly, or tennis, while all of us are forced to obey the law, like it or not, agree with it or not. Moreover, in the real world the stakes are not mere pride or Monopoly money, but control over our very lives, from cradle to grave. What we are after is a set of principles that, if adhered to, will guarantee that we can accept the distribution of the fruits of social cooperation, whatever that pattern happens to be. The idea is just like Magie's: we try out alternative sets of rules, hypothetically, and see which makes for the better game.

Let's return to an earlier thought. Suppose we could start a society from scratch, as we might a business. The business is meant to generate primary goods and to continue doing so in perpetuity. There is no intention for our enterprise ever to shut down and wind up its affairs. Generation after generation is expected to continue the business. What would a charter look like (and here we suppose there is no standing body of business law to refer to)?

At the threshold, the charter would have to specify two things about the enterprise. The first is how to capitalize it. The second is how decisions are to be made. For the purpose of abstracting from the variety and complexity of human psychology, let's say a soloist's one aim is to maximize the package of primary goods available to her (and her near and dear). She is not directly concerned with what others get. She looks only to what she can expect in absolute terms. She is not interested in having a greater supply relative to others.

In other words, soloists are not spiteful or envious. A soloist is not going to take less than she might otherwise have merely for the purpose of making things tougher for others. Likewise, a soloist is not willing to take less merely in order to assure that no one gets more than she does. A soloist is not a rigid egalitarian: she is not attracted to the idea that the better-off be leveled-down simply to make everyone equal, the way the legendary Procrustes sawed off the legs of his guests to the length of his own bed.

The investment capital that each person puts in will not include their bodies or minds, but it will include what is produced due to their common efforts. The business retains its ongoing earnings, net of what it distributes to each as needed to elicit her productive effort. It conserves resources to the extent it calculates to be needed to be fair to later generations.

Incomes are determined by a market for labor. Those who have talents in short supply might earn more. Those who prefer leisure can expect to earn less. As long as the rules governing the enterprise are fair ones, and are observed, then no one can justly complain that others earn more or have more. To what standard could a complainer appeal?

Decisions have to be made about how to allocate what is owned in common, and what restrictions and levies there are to be on private property. In fact, decisions have to be made about what kinds of thing can and cannot be privately owned. A soloist will insist that all who wish it will have an equal say in all these decisions. The basic charter will call for a liberal democratic decision process. It will specify what is beyond the legitimate scope of the enterprise's authority. What is within that scope is subject to the principle of majority rule. The basic charter is the social contract. It is complete when it specifies these things. It need not specify more, for its purpose is to state a standard for judging whether the enterprise is operating justly.

The question that heads this chapter – Why economic inequality? – can now be answered. There is no natural law that decrees that all should hold equal shares in everything (or if there is such a law, there is no chance that everyone will believe it). There is no prospect of an objectively impeccable, incontestable way to measure each individual's marginal contribution to society. Actual market outcomes are measurable with a good degree of objectivity – but are they just? Does the market give each her due? The justice of a given distribution of holdings can only be affirmed where we can show that the labor market operates within a framework of basic institutions that no one could reasonably object to.

It would be unreasonable to insist upon an equal distribution if an unequal distribution would make everyone in society better off. What, other than envy, could motivate someone to insist on an equal division of a lesser whole when a certain, accessible unequal division would mean not only a greater whole but greater-sized shares for all? (Of course, the soloist will want to review the charter she derives in light of the psychological reality of spite and envy, and the evidence of socially corrosive effects of economic inequality – but it will be helpful to derive principles first that are not themselves shaped by spite or envy.)

A soloist is not spiteful or envious; so a soloist prefers "efficient" changes, that is, changes that leave no one worse off while making some people (and not necessarily all) better off. What she objects to, though, is the idea of having to accept less for herself, in absolute terms, merely in order that others can get more. She does not care that she is made *relatively* worse off, in material terms, so long as the basic structure of society assures her equality in the things that she will insist on having an equal share of.

We have already noted some of the things a soloist will insist on having an equal share of. One of them is equal liberty of conscience. The soloist insists on strict equality in this instance. The soloist insists on having this liberty in the greatest possible measure, consistent with others' enjoying the same liberty. This measure will be one of equality: the greatest liberty of conscience a soloist can reasonably hope for can be no greater than what she is willing to allow all others.

Moreover, the soloist recognizes that letting others have a greater liberty of conscience than she has cannot result in her having a greater liberty of conscience. Freedom of conscience isn't like other primary goods such as wealth. It is plausible to say to someone, "*You will have more wealth if you permit others to hold wealth greater than yours*: there will be a bigger pie and your slice, though smaller than theirs, will be larger than an equal slice of a smaller pie." Try paraphrasing that remark, substituting "liberty of conscience" for "wealth." The result of the substitution makes no sense. There is no conceivable way that someone else's enjoying greater religious liberty than mine could lead to my having greater religious liberty than I would otherwise have had. Liberty of conscience doesn't work that way. That's one reason it has a priority over other liberties.

There is another limit to a soloist's willingness to tolerate relative inequality of wealth and the advantages that go with it. This has to do with the opportunities society offers: such as careers, education, and self-development. These should be open to all, equally, without regard to sex or race or other irrelevant or immutable personal traits. A soloist recognizes that it would be unreasonable to propose principles that favor one sex or favor one race, because a principle that was discriminatory in that way could reasonably be rejected by anyone who happened to be of that sex or race.

A formal nondiscrimination principle, with respect to careers and opportunities, is not enough to satisfy her. Opportunities for education and occupation ought to be the same for persons who have the same native talent and ambition. Those children whose families are wealthy and well-connected ought not to have a head start in the competition for the best schools and the best-paid and most prestigious jobs.

But why shouldn't they? We, evidently, were born into a society in which what each winds up with is strongly correlated with what he had to start with, thanks to his family situation. Family situations can vary enormously, yet two things seem fairly constant. One, most households that have children strive to do the best they can for these children, and especially for theirs above all others. Two, many households work hard to provide lifetime advantages for their children – advantages that are additional to what the average child would have.

Why would we not choose to be born into a society governed by a principle that guaranteed formal equality of opportunity and left it at that? Wouldn't we want to be born into a society in which households and parents are given an incentive to make special efforts to advantage their own? Or would it be irrational to choose such a principle if one lacked prior knowledge that one would be born better off than others? A soloist might want to chance this, if the circumstances were such that she was assured of not being too badly off even if she did turn out not to be among the well-born. It might be an exciting gamble. If the downside is bearable, and the upside is huge, it would be irrational not to take a chance.

The downside might be bearable if two things are guaranteed: one, the equal basic liberties are secure; and, two, there is a social minimum of material means that is also secure. To insist on a social minimum, or safety net, is to reject the proposal to organize society according to a winner-takes-all principle. Under winner-takes-all, those who find themselves out of work, for whatever reason – injury, sickness, failing demand for their skills – have to provide for themselves. And if they cannot, then they have to beg, borrow, or steal. Stealing, of course, will land them in jail (without passing "Go"). And failing to pay their debts will result in their beggary.

A soloist's temperament is opposed to accepting charity, and is fiercely opposed to asking for it. A soloist expects to be able to stand on her own two feet and to accept responsibility for her decisions, including her career decisions. If she chose to become an elevator operator or a stenographer, then tough. Even so, on reflection, a soloist will recognize that she is vulnerable in countless ways that cannot entirely be foreseen, or prepared for, if she does not enlist others. She does not want charity, but at the same time, if she is forced into an enterprise in partnership with others, and her only say about it has to be in the form of a vote on its governing rules, the rational calculator in her will want to propose some kind of social insurance.

A soloist will want to insist on a social minimum for another reason. She wants peace and stability in her transactions with others. She can be brought to trust others to keep their promises, but not if she can tell they have over-promised. A person reduced to beggary cannot be counted on to resist the strains of committing to the rules that define and protect private property.

Suppose the social minimum is included in the social contract. (Welcome to the Andrew Yang gang!) The equal basic liberties are secure and there is a social dividend of material means that is also secure. Surely, now, it would be preferable to be born into a society governed by the "families first" principle, provided it is a liberal society with a decent social safety net? Isn't it exciting to daydream about being born into posh circumstances? It needn't be a lonely existence, one could have posh friends among the children of the posh parents one's own parents mix and mingle with.

A soloist is not one to be "downcast by the greater fortunes of others," as long as she has her due. Her due, in a "family first" society, consists in her basic liberties, a social minimum, and whatever wealth and income she realizes due to her own efforts building upon the advantages and beneficence of those near and dear to her, especially her parents and grandparents.

Upon reflection, a soloist might start to worry about the ongoing stability of a family-first society. She will wonder how a family-first society will provide for social mobility. If bright and motivated children are born to or placed in families that cannot afford the best schools, and tutors, and so on, these children will have more trouble advancing than they would if they did have those advantages.

Talented children stuck in less interesting and fulfilling jobs than the brilliant careers they might have had can turn into trouble as they mature. They might justly resent the fact that others, though no more talented or diligent, get a head start in life that catapults them even further ahead. A soloist might think of herself as a trustee for such a child, for that child might be herself, or one of her own.

A principle of fair equality of opportunity would guarantee that chances for opportunities and occupations are roughly the same for young people having the same aptitude and motivation, irrespective of family wealth and connections. The family-first principle, by contrast, allows the wealthy and well-connected to parlay their own advantages into further advantages for their children and other relations. Were she choosing between a family-first principle, and a principle of fair equality of opportunity, which would it be?

A soloist can feel torn here. She likes to think of herself as self-defining and self-made, proud and independent, capable of standing on her own two feet. If she has children, she hopes to impart to them the same sturdy ethic she lives by herself. On the other hand, she sees nothing wrong with parents wanting their kids to have the best of everything. Especially, the best of those things which, by their very nature, are things that not every child, nor even every worthy child, can have.

At this point, the soloist should ask whether the tension she feels should be resolved by the democratic process. Getting unanimous consent to either of the competing principles – family-first or fair equality of opportunity – looks unlikely. There could be some intermediate principle yet to be articulated that no one could reasonably reject. What might it be, though? Why not let the majority decide, instead, as a matter of everyday legislation? That way, if a law proves unworkable, it can be amended as many times as the majority sees fit. From now on, let's say the soloist accepts a *principle of equality of opportunity*, full stop – with the understanding that she accepts the necessity of legislative balancing between families-first and fair equality of opportunity.

Majority rule will have to decide a myriad of things anyway: what is the budget for education, how is it to be funded, where are schools to be built, what credentials (if any) should teachers have, and how much are they to be paid, etc. The soloist will accept the legislature's decision on these matters even when she disagrees. This is because she accepts the justice of the basic structure and recognizes that it has to enable the majority to decide those matters that are within the scope of the state's legitimate authority. The basic structure will feature a liberal democratic decision-making process, which gives her an equal say in the decisions reached.

Her certainty of her political equality reconciles the soloist to the justice of the level of economic inequality her society allows, whatever it turns out to be. She now has to ask, what assurance of political equality is there in this social contract put in front of her (figuratively speaking) to sign? It had better be solid.

3

How Much Economic Inequality?

Our question has been this: when we conceive of society itself as a fair cooperative venture for mutual benefit, what principle should govern how the goods it makes possible are to be divided? The basic structure of society is not stable unless it is possible to appeal to a public standard to settle disputes about justice. Those who regard the basic structure as unjust can, of course, be coerced into compliance with its rules. A soloist would resent such coercion, and would not want to have to depend upon it as the answer to herself or to others as to matters of basic justice.

Political states have always resorted to force to maintain order; but a soloist wants it understood that force is the last resort. Government can hardly be said to rest on the consent of the governed if force is conspicuous, or readily deployed, when citizens have grievances. A society is stable for the right reasons when there is a social contract that can be appealed to as a guide to assessing the justice of the institutions making up its basic structure, which includes its economy.

In the preceding chapters, it was shown that a soloist will insist upon certain inviolable basic rights, as terms of any social contract she would agree to and trust others to adhere to. These rights must be held equally. Even so, a soloist accepts that the wealth that a cooperative society makes possible need not be shared equally. In fact, it would be irrational to insist on equal shares if significantly greater wealth would be created by permitting economic incentives.

More fundamentally, a soloist accepts that efforts deserve to be rewarded, and that she, and everyone else, has a right to decide what occupation to pursue and how much leisure time to enjoy. All must participate, who can, in the labor market. But all will rightly insist upon choosing what role to accept and, up to a point, how much effort to put into it.

Consider this case. Helga is a pulmonologist, a medical doctor who specializes in lung ailments. She earns more than Walter, a nurse on her ward, even though both work the same number of hours and do their jobs equally well. An economy that allows this inequality need not be condemned as unjust. Helga may have incurred extra expenses to acquire the specialized skills she has. Let's suppose, though, that both Walter and Helga received all their training at public expense.

Walter wants to know why he is paid less than Helga. It is likely that Helga has spent years longer training to be a pulmonologist. What would induce Helga to spend those extra years in training, if not the prospect of earning more money? True, Helga might be compensated by the additional prestige enjoyed by specialists. How would that be conveyed? And wouldn't Walter resent that inequality as well?

Allowing monetary incentives has a number of advantages over non-monetary ones; and both have advantages over the exclusion of incentives. Consider also this. Suppose Helga practices in a locality whose population has been increasing rapidly. Her employer would like for her to work additional hours to help cover the additional demand. Helga would rather spend those hours gardening. If Helga refuses to work additional hours without compensation, surely she is within her rights. She stands upon her basic right to decide how much leisure she wants to set aside for herself, as a contributing member of society. For the same reason, Helga should have the right to negotiate the rate of compensation for surrendering her leisure time.

Now, many socialists would condemn Helga's attitude, and go on to condemn any economic system that would accommodate it. From their perspective, Helga should be willing to provide freely "according to her ability." Helga should also be ashamed to demand any more than the absolute minimum she would take as compensation. Experience, however, has shown that society is less productive if it tries to eliminate monetary incentives and the inequalities that necessarily result.

The Soviet Union tried to substitute medals for money, and lauded Stakhanovite workers who exceeded their unit's output quota. This experiment did not work out well. Planners increased the unit quotas. The Stakhanovites began to be resented by their comrades. Medals accumulated, but not more quickly than resentful, sidelong looks. Demand for consumer goods went unexpressed (and hence unsatisfied) in the official market. The joke took hold, "We pretend to work, and they pretend to pay us."

A soloist is also aware that the value of her basic liberties is affected by the amount of money she can spend to pursue her idea of the good life. Therefore, in accepting economic inequality, she has to reconcile herself to the fact that the liberty to go surfing in Jeffreys Bay, in Newquay, or off Malibu, for example, will be worth less to her if she chooses to be a nurse rather than a pulmonologist.

Equal liberty does not equate to equal *worth* of liberty. There is a principle of responsibility that she accepts: if she has expensive tastes, it is up to her to earn the money to indulge them. It is not an injustice if society makes her pay her own way in the pursuit of fulfillment of her personal tastes. It is not unjust if the social minimum that she will insist upon does not cover them. This principle of responsibility applies to other basic liberties as well. Liberty of conscience can be enjoyed by the better-off financially over a wider range of faiths. The better-off can afford to pay for indulgences and pilgrimages that the less well-off cannot.

What a soloist will insist on, though, is that the economy operate in a way that benefits everyone who is part of it. This means that the inequalities between different classes of citizen should never be at the expense of the lower classes.

Do skip ahead if the following illustration is superfluous, but a soloist will form a definite order of preferences among the three economies represented in Table 1.

The economies are those of three distinct societies, 1, 2, and 3. Each society is divided into two representative classes, A and B. Units of goods are distributed as indicated between the two classes, and totaled up in the right-hand column. The soloist can choose which of the three societies she would like to belong to, but she cannot pick which of the two classes, A or B, she will land in within that society. She does not know the sizes of the two classes. Assume the equal basic liberties are guaranteed in any case.

The soloist will prefer Society 2 to Society 1. That is because she is concerned only with how well-off she is. She will be better off in Society 2, whichever class she winds up belonging to. For the same reason, she will prefer Society 3 to Society 1, despite the fact that the inequality between the two classes is fairly stark. Again, as we have been stipulating, she is not envious of those doing better than she, so long as she is doing better compared to the alternative. Class B does much better than class A in Society 3, but class A in Society 3 does better than either class in Society 1. We have another illustration of a main reason why a soloist will not be a strict egalitarian.

TABLE 1

	Class A	Class B	Total
Society 1	100	100	200
Society 2	115	120	235
Society 3	110	140	250

The interesting question is what preference a soloist has as between Society 2 and Society 3. The soloist is unimpressed with the fact that total wealth is greater in Society 3 than in Society 2. She takes the viewpoint of the less-advantaged or least-advantaged representative member, and asks, which Society maximizes the goods held by that person? The answer to that question is not Society 3, but Society 2. The less-advantaged representative person in Society 2 can expect to do better than the less-advantaged in Society 3.

This assumes that the soloist does not know the probabilities of her belonging to one class or the other in the three societies. If she knows she will likely be in the best-off class in whatever society she belongs to, she should choose Society 3, because the better-off do best in that society. Likewise, if she is excited by the opportunity to have a shot at having the most goods she possibly can, she might choose Society 3. We have assumed that the soloist is not a risk-seeker (or risk-averse). This assumption about soloist psychology makes sense, though. Suppose there is one more society to compare, Society 4, in which the jackpot is huge.

In Society 4, the chooser has a chance to be 100 units better off than in Society 3. And, also, a chance to be 100 units worse off than in the worse outcome in Society 3. For a gambling-minded soloist, Casino 4 – ahem – *Society* 4 is where the action is. But under what circumstances would it be rational for a soloist who was risk-neutral rather than risk-seeking to be indifferent between Society 3 and Society 4?

TABLE 2

	Class A	Class B	Total
Society 1	100	100	200
Society 2	115	120	235
Society 3	110	140	250
Society 4	10	240	250

True, where the probabilities of landing in Class A or Class B are unknown, the soloist might assign each placement a .5 probability, and in that case the "expected value" of joining Society 3 is the same as that of joining Society 4. Even so, unless 10 units amounts to an already very, *very* satisfactory helping of goods, it should strike a soloist as irrational to risk joining Society 4 rather than Society 3.

Remember, also, that the soloist's question is not, which society to join, but which society she would prefer to have been forced into, Society 3 or Society 4? If she finds that she belongs to Class A, her allegiance to the rules of Society 4 will rightly be under suspicion if it is known that *she* knows Society 3 is an option denied to her. The under-class in Society 3 is on average 100 units better off, and if every unit counts to her, she might rightly resent having to live by the rules of Society 4. She might even think of herself and her class as having been robbed of 100 units. Sounds like Hobbes's "precincts of battalle."

The choice between Society 2 and Society 3 has the same structure, from the perspective of those in Class A. The less-advantaged representative person in Society 3 can expect to do better than the less-advantaged in Society 4, and so also the less-advantaged in Society 2 can expect to do better than the less-advantaged in Society 3. The less-advantaged can rightly resent being forced to live by Society 3 rules rather than Society 2 rules, just as the less-advantaged in Society 4 could rightly resent being forced to play by Society 4 rules rather than Society 3 rules. The only difference is that the arbitrary numbers assigned make the loss to the less-advantaged under Society 4 rules look more dramatic. In both comparisons, the less-advantaged are forced to accept less in order that the more advantaged may have more.

Because Society 2 rules are an option, rules of the Society 3 and Society 4 sort cannot be part of a social contract that is stable for the right reasons: the less-advantaged can be forced to play, but they cannot be counted on to do so solely because they see the justice of the game. They don't see the rules as designed to serve their pursuit of the good.

Resentment for being forced to take less so others can have more can cut both ways, though. The better-off under Society 3 rules get 20 units less under Society 2 rules, in order that the less well-off can get 5 units more. As between Society 2 and Society 3, someone will have grounds for resentment. Why is the resentment of the less-well-off decisive, from a soloist point of view?

Suppose the soloist would rather choose between the two on the basis of average expectation. Assume the population is the same between Society 2 and Society 3, and the membership of the two classes is not too heavily skewed toward the less-advantaged, then it would follow that the average expectation in Society 3 is higher than that in Society 2. This is because the total number of units in Society 3 is greater: it is the wealthier society. Why wouldn't a soloist prefer to choose on that basis?

The answer here could be that the soloist is mindful of the strains of commitment upon others. *Ex ante*, as they say in ECON 101, the rational thing to do is to maximize expected utility, if we can assume that no outcome is unbearable. We have already assumed that the basic liberties are guaranteed in each of these hypothetical societies. The less-advantaged can never be the mere property of the more-advantaged. The problem is that, *ex post*, when the less-advantaged discover their situation, they might find it impossible to accept, knowing that they have been forced to live under rules that allow their group less and others more. Of course, again, the more-advantaged too might chafe under rules that keep them from receiving as much as they would under Society 3 rules – having to sacrifice, as it were, solely so that the less-advantaged not feel put-upon. The better-off might also point to the greater total wealth – GDP! – under Society 3 rules.

It looks to be a standoff. We can reformulate the competing ideas as stating two alternative principles by which to assess the distribution of wealth and income.

Restricted Utility Principle: once the equal basic liberties, equality of opportunity, and a decent social minimum are assured, the distribution of wealth and income is just if the institutions of the basic structure of society manifestly serve to maximize *average wealth*.

Restricted Difference Principle: once the equal basic liberties, equality of opportunity, and a decent social minimum are assured, the distribution of wealth and income is just if the institutions of the basic structure of society manifestly serve to maximize *the wealth of the least-advantaged*.

Now, egalitarians, socialists, and others will be quick to point out that both of these principles leave open the possibility of enormous economic inequality. As long as the institutions making up the basic structure manifestly serve to increase a certain measure (the "maximand"), then justice is done under either of these two principles. Under the Restricted Utility Principle, the maximand is average wealth. Under the Restricted Difference Principle, it is the wealth of the least-advantaged class. Both allow otherwise unrestricted economic inequality: neither principle sets any cap on relative economic inequality. Both guarantee equal basic rights, in a formal sense, but make the unequal worth of those rights a matter of personal responsibility (if you want to go on a surfing safari off Malibu, get to work).

A soloist will have to confess that she can come up with no principled limit to the degree of allowable economic inequality in a society, once the implications of liberty and the advantages of incentives are taken on board. Some extreme ratios between the holdings of the better-off and the worse-off will stand out as disturbing, even shocking. Even so, if the equal basic liberties are assured, and there is equality of opportunity, and a decent social safety net, who can complain?

Inevitably, some will complain, but on what ground?

On the ground of injustice? Or can the complainers be dismissed on the ground that they have consented to take part in a system that operates by rules that do not attempt the impossible: that is, they do not attempt to hold every pattern of distribution up to scrutiny, on a case-by-case basis. And they do not attempt to cap the degree of relative inequality at some arbitrary ratio. What would that ratio be? 3 to 1? Why not 5 to 1? Or 10 to 1, the post-WWII norm in Japan and the Scandinavian countries?

Empirical research might point to some certain ratio beyond which other indicators of social well-being tend to decline (see Wilkinson and Pickett 2010). Yet it seems implausible to say that everyone is entitled, as a matter of *justice*, to live in the happiest society possible. A soloist insists upon her basic liberties even though she realizes they come at a cost.

Strict inequality is unreasonable, for the reasons already discussed. No plausible, principled limit to the relative degree of material inequality can be stated. By a round-about path, we come back to the idea that a stable social contract should be one that states a publicly available criterion under which citizens can accept the pattern of distribution as just, whatever it is. It can be seen as just because it results from rules defining processes that can be accepted as just.

Haven't we already got such a process in place, if the equal basic liberties include equal political rights in a democracy? As long as the basic institutions of society are governed democratically, the inequalities of wealth and opportunity that arise can be limited and corrected to the degree and in the manner the majority sees fit. If each has an equal say, and if the institutions making up the basic structure manifest that either average wealth or the wealth of the least-advantaged class would be lower if the distribution were more equal, who can complain of social injustice? If the degree of economic inequality we find in society still troubles us, it could be a clue that something has gone wrong at a more fundamental level.

4

How Much Political Equality?

The equal political rights are a set of related rights. Some of them are general rights that also apply to the political sphere. These include freedom of speech, assembly, and association. Soloists demand the right to speak their minds on any subject whatever, be it sports, religion, politics, or popular culture. Soloists adamantly defend their right to choose their associates, whether to form a book club, a subreddit, or an advocacy group. Soloists will peacefully gather as they please in public spaces, whether to watch a street performance or to hold a noisy demonstration.

Other political rights are distinctive to the democratic process. The right to vote is preeminent, and a soloist will insist that hers be an equal vote, in matters that concern her. What the polity itself decides is always at least potentially of concern to her, because its decisions normally are costly to her in some degree, in that they limit her liberty and are coercively enforced by the public power.

Elections are typically the focal point of a national democratic process. People tend to hate math and love numbers. Numbers mean that news media can easily script their material in a dramatic format, from the countdown to election day, the pre-election polls and vote projections, the vote-counts as returns come in, the projections of winners and losers, all culminating in declaring the winners, and counting up wins and losses for parties, and so forth.

The importance of casting and counting up votes will not distract the soloist from other essential aspects of democracy. It matters who and what is on the ballot, and it matters whether the winning proposal is carried out and enforced as law, and whether the winning candidate is installed in office. A process cannot be judged as democratic, or not, in the abstract. A club might be run democratically, and give each member a vote. That does not mean it is a democracy including the janitor, who scrubs the floors and cleans the toilets in the clubhouse. A soloist will not regard a state as legitimately governing her, as a citizen, unless she is included in a democratic process by which it makes laws and regulations.

A process is not democratic with respect to those who have no say in it.

At its founding, the United States of America was democratic as to qualified free, white, propertied male adults, but it was a dictatorship as to everyone else. The United Kingdom over centuries has become more democratic, in the sense that it has extended the voting franchise to previously excluded classes. What was to become the Soviet Union was, at its founding, democratic as to members of socialist parties, but was a dictatorship as to everyone else. It degenerated into the dictatorship of a single party, the Communist Party. Non-party members could vote in elections, but the Party decided on the candidates. Before long, the Party was not a democracy even as to its own membership. The Soviet Union was not a democracy, despite the elections it ran. These elections, with their huge, compulsory turnouts, were rightly scorned as a sham by critics in the West.

So, a soloist will regard a government as governing her by consent only if it is democratic *as to her*. If some subject is important to her, she must have a say in what measures to address it are put to a vote; and this entails that she must be able to call for a vote on measures she would like to have voted on. Is she making unrealistic demands? Does she reject the legitimacy of representative democracy? Not necessarily. What matters to her is that she have an equal say in choosing representatives and in holding them accountable for what they do and fail to do. It matters that she has an equal right to stand for election as a representative, and that, if elected, she have the same rights as any other representative to introduce proposals for a vote.

A soloist is realistic about the limits of democracy. She is bound to obey the laws of foreign countries when she visits, despite having no political rights. But she rightly refuses to be ruled as an alien in her own country. She knows she has to follow the work-rules in the place where she works, even when decisions about them are made unilaterally by managers and not democratically or by collective bargaining. Many socialists insist that democracy belongs here, too, as a matter of justice – let's postpone this question until Chapter 8.

In any case, it is clear that there must always be room for voluntary associations, including churches that do not conduct themselves along democratic lines. Congregationalist congregations, for example, are democratic. Yet Roman Catholic churches are emphatically not run democratically, as to their members. A Catholic soloist acknowledges that she has chosen to be governed by priests, as to matters of religious doctrine and practice. If she doesn't like it, she is free to find another denomination. But she insists that the nation she calls home governs legitimately only by her consent. Her failure to emigrate does not constitute her consent. Her consent can be implied only if the nation's constitution consists of principles she cannot reasonably refuse to acknowledge as the measure of justice. In other words, a country that is hers is governed by and under a social contract to which all reasonable citizens can be said to consent.

At this point, a doubt has to be raised and addressed. It is this. A soloist will not insist upon, or accept, a social contract that imposes strict economic equality. She accepts the justice of a system that differentially rewards efforts and talents, for the reason that such a system need leave nobody worse off and everyone, or many, better off, in absolute terms. She also accepts that there is no principled way, no way that nobody could reasonably reject, of assessing the society-wide distribution of wealth from moment to moment; and that there is no principled numerical cap that be put on the allowed ratio of the holdings of the best-off to the holdings of the least-well-off.

A soloist will insist on strict equality of certain rights – conscience, speech, and bodily integrity, for example – but she accepts that the usefulness, or worth, of those rights will not be the same for everyone. Those with more wealth, income, and other material resources will be able more freely to pursue their ends than those who have less in the way of those resources. The soloist proudly accepts a principle of responsibility: she must trim her desires to fit her budget, and cultivate those tastes she can afford to indulge. This is a necessary consequence of accepting the permissibility of incentives. If Helga the pulmonologist knows her every desire will be well-funded whether or not she works those extra hours, what's her incentive to do so?

Now comes the question, is merely formal equality of political liberties enough? Or will a soloist insist on the equal worth of these liberties (though only of these)? The problem with being contented with merely formal political equality can be readily seen. If, say, Helga the pulmonologist wants to buy a vintage bottle of wine that Walter the wine-loving nurse cannot afford, the soloist has settled into the opinion that the formal equal liberty to buy a bottle of that vintage is all that justice requires.

If Wazir, another pulmonologist, is Muslim, and wants to visit Mecca to perform the *hajj*, he may do so without having to cut back on any of his other pursuits. Another nurse, Nour, in the same situation can afford to perform the *hajj* also, but only by cutting back on other pursuits. But suppose Helga the pulmonologist and Walter the nurse are competing for a seat on the city council. The fact that

Helga will spend more on the race than the nurse seems troubling in a way not evident in the other cases.

The reason the city-council case is more troubling than the *hajj* case or the vintage-wine case is that the soloist was looking to the democratic political process as the guarantee that inequality of wealth would not grow to an intolerable degree. An extreme degree of economic inequality could destabilize society and dissolve the social contract. Society is supposed to be conceived as a fair cooperative venture for mutual benefit. The rewards are supposed to benefit everyone (at least on average), compared to all feasible alternative distributions – or at least to seem to do so. But that appearance, much less the reality, increasingly dissolves as inequalities that are extraneous to political competence are permitted to determine the *worth* of political liberty.

A soloist acknowledges that political competence is possessed by different people in different degrees. Acknowledging others as one's political equal does not entail the fiction that all are equally competent in their political judgments. Political competence comprises a variety of traits. These include intelligence, open-mindedness, empathy, information, motivation, and other qualities of mind and character.

These traits are possessed in different proportions by different people. It is highly unlikely that general agreement could be reached as to the optimal mix of such traits. It is almost certain that the average person considers herself to be above average in her possession of at least some of these component traits. Even people who consider themselves to be utterly apolitical are unlikely to have that attitude on the basis of a self-awareness that they lack, say, sufficiently sound judgment.

A soloist can also acknowledge that achievement that is rewarded monetarily correlates to some degree with some of the traits that make up political competence. An informed city-council member should be able to make sense of a balance-sheet. So also, a voter who can make sense of a balance-sheet is better able to detect a candidate's deficiency in that department.

Acknowledging these facts might suggest limiting the voting franchise to electors who can pass an examination that tests these traits. Obviously, it would be controversial what relative weight to assign to the various traits, to say nothing of the difficulty of administering the exam. What about giving every adult one vote, and allotting extra votes for, say, college graduates? (A proposal floated by soloist icon John Stuart Mill.)

The soloist might not be repelled by the notion; however, she knows that it invites controversy. How many extra votes should the college graduates get? Only one? One for each year of study? Each semester? Etc. Moreover, she knows that those without college degrees would rightly resent their exclusion. Why would those lacking some magical piece of paper accept the legitimacy of laws made by processes that presume that they are inferior in political competence?

Suppose Helga the pulmonologist has handled the business side of her practice, or in some other way accumulated a track-record indicating her business acumen, while Walter the nurse has no such record. Surely this fact is relevant to a voter's judgment as to the relative political competence of the pulmonologist and the nurse as candidates for the city council. What seems to the soloist to be utterly irrelevant is the fact that Helga has more money to spend on her candidacy. Wealth, and the ability to raise money, are not themselves components of political competence. Nor are they promising proxies for any element of political competence.

Economic inequality can negate the equal worth of the political liberties. The soloist will insist that any two citizens, at any given level of political competence, have roughly the same political power, regardless of their relative wealth and social connections. Merely formal political equality is not enough – in fact, it can disguise a failure of democracy in democratic dress.

The soloist has to weigh two arguments in favor of allowing unequal wealth to express itself freely in the political arena.

One argument is that it would be irrational for a soloist to insist on even formal political equality if, without it, she would be compensated by having more wealth, which in turn would enhance the worth to her of her non-political basic liberties. She could make the *hajj*, or buy that vintage wine, if only the experts were left to run the government and the economy. Why would the soloist obsess about having a say, when the say she would have is practically negligible, and not having it frees those who know best to steer the ship of state?

This argument will not impress the soloist. Apart from its unwarranted assumption that such experts and expertise exist, it comes too late. Millions of non-experts are accustomed to having formally equal voting rights. The social contract must at least honor these promises.

The second argument is that the soloist should be contented with her formal political equality. She has her vote. She is free to cast it as she pleases. The wealthy have the same one vote she has: one person, one vote. It may be true that she cannot afford to run for office, while others with no greater political competence can afford to. It may be true that she cannot afford to buy tickets for the fundraisers for political candidates, while others with no more political competence than she has can afford them. That's tough.

She should accept responsibility for her having a taste she cannot afford. She should work harder, be cleverer, earn more money, invest shrewdly, and (with luck) she will be able to afford to donate to that candidate (or go on that *hajj*, or buy that vintage bottle). She should take responsibility for each of these choices – nothing stands in her way, formally.

The soloist will approach this argument in the way suggested earlier. Suppose she and a group of others were forced to cooperate in order to survive some dire situation.

They are castaways on a desert island, say. A basic agreement must be reached to lay out the ground rules for the venture, and this will include agreement on a decision-making procedure. The procedural rules must be agreed to unanimously, but circumstances compel unanimous agreement to a procedure by which a less-than-unanimous vote will suffice to settle the issues properly raised. What would motivate the castaways to allow those who became wealthier over time to leverage that advantage into advantages in the decision-making process?

One motive might be to gain that kind of advantage for oneself. One might want a chance to supplement the influence flowing from exercising one's political competence, with the ultimate aim of putting through proposals that would otherwise have less chance of passage. Of course, for this to make sense, one would have to be counting on becoming wealthier than others. Fixing the rules in order to leverage one's supposed advantages is not likely to impress others as a way to set up a just procedure. Others will suspect that the wealthier, who are freely able to use their wealth to influence political outcomes, are doing so precisely to achieve outcomes that (further) favor the wealthy. Over time, further unequal accumulation cannot confidently be accounted to the need to incentivize effort, innovation, and skills-development.

The social contract that allows economic inequality freely to affect the political process is unstable. It is unstable because those with less political influence, but equal political competence, rightly resent being forced to live by rules they can reasonably reject as systematically biased to favor an already-favored class.

The same complaint cannot be made against allowing those with greater political competence to have greater political influence. Those who take an interest in politics, and expend the energy needed to command the issues, ought to have greater influence (other things being equal). Political decisions should be competently made. The less-wealthy, however, have no reason to think that the wealthy, as a class, are more public spirited or wiser or fairer-minded than anyone else. Nor could the wealthy very convincingly pretend otherwise.

On behalf of the wealthy, it might be argued that, because they have more wealth, they have more to lose, and because they have more to lose, they can safely be presumed to take greater care in exercising what political competence they possess than those who, though equally competent, lack wealth. The answer to this argument was implicit in a remark made at Putney by the English Agitator, Captain Rainsborough, in the mid-seventeenth century, when he said, "the poorest *he* that is in England has a life to live as the richest *he*." Those who are without property are the least able to afford careless government.

In sum, the wealthy cannot reasonably insist that they be permitted to spend freely to influence political outcomes. The wealthy – and this includes those who aspire to wealth – cannot reasonably expect others to submit to coercively enforceable decisions in which those others had less than an effectively, as well as formally, equal say.

The political liberties are different from the other basic liberties. As to those others, it is not unreasonable to apply a principle of responsibility. If, for example, the freedom to travel to exotic destinations is worth less to you than it is to your rich neighbor, then your remedy is to earn and save. There is more wealth, and hence greater average wealth, if material incentives are reflected through the operation of a labor market. If the social contract includes the Restricted Difference Principle, instead of the Restricted Utility Principle, then the basic structure is such that only those economic inequalities that increase the wealth of all classes of society are allowed.

Under either principle, economic inequalities that it would be unreasonable to disallow are automatically reflected in the unequal worth of the non-political basic liberties. Those who earn more get to keep more, and thus get to spend more and travel more.

Political influence is a good that does not operate

the same way other goods do. My traveling more does not mean your traveling less. In fact, my traveling more might expand the opportunities you have to travel. In a market society, greater demand for most goods leads to an expanded and more affordable supply of those goods. Political influence is not like travel. It is a good thing to have political influence, but my having more of it does not lead to your having more. It is the reverse. My having more means your having less (even if you happen to agree with me on everything). There are winners and losers in politics.

Moreover, my spending to enhance my political influence does not tend to make political influence more affordable for you. Again, it is the reverse. If I buy a $5000 ticket for a candidate's fundraising dinner, that does not mean that the candidate is any likelier to sell $5 tickets too. The candidate might be happy to take your $5 donation, but you can bet that it will not get you the same access, and the same chance to influence the candidate, that I have.

Even to say that your $5 gets you a thousandth of the influence I've bought is to exaggerate. In America today, candidates for important offices like the U.S. Senate routinely sell expensive supporter "packages" for graduated amounts, bearing names like "Investor," "Shareholder," and "Stakeholder." Do not be insulted if I state the obvious: this free market for political influence does not tend to "raise all boats."

A liberal democratic social contract forbids the marketing of certain goods. Bribery and vote-buying are punishable under every criminal code, even codes of illiberal or undemocratic regimes, because they are so obviously inimical to a social contract. In the next chapter, we will ask whether there are any other markets a social contract must forbid. For the moment, it is enough to note that, whatever else is for sale, political influence ought not to be.

A soloist will naturally want it to be understood that she cannot consent to be governed by a regime in which she has any less than an effectively equal say in what the legal rules will be. This equality of effect is of course dependent upon the degree to which she takes an interest in politics, and how informed and persuasive she is. It should not be diminished or enhanced merely on account of how much money she has to spend. It is unjust if a wealthier person has a greater influence on the determination of a political issue, solely on account of having greater wealth. It is unjust because it is unreasonable to expect that anyone would consent to such an arrangement unless she was already rich or expected to be.

"Justice is what is in the interest of the stronger" is no principle of justice. It would be irrational for anyone but the strong to propose. And it would be unreasonable for the stronger to expect anyone less strong to obey it. By the same token, "Let political power vary according to wealth" is not a clause anyone would propose to others, as a term of the social contract, unless she was persuaded of one of two things.

She might be persuaded that she would become wealthier than others, as the social enterprise progressed. In this case, she could not reasonably expect others to assent to a rule designed to their disadvantage. Alternatively, she might be persuaded that everyone would be better off under a plutocracy. The evidence for such a belief is scant. History seems to demonstrate that plutocracies are unstable. Social and economic inequality increase under plutocratic rule, as the rich tend to fortify and extend their advantages. There is no reason to hope such an arrangement can end well, unless there is some reason to think that political competence increases with increasing wealth. Examples to the contrary are too numerous, and too notorious, to need mention.

Summary of Part One

Our soloist wants to live peaceably in society with others. She knows that peace is precarious if it is seen as an unjust imposition by the more powerful. Peace is unstable unless it is more than a mere hiatus, or a strategic cease-fire during which contending forces strive to improve their position for the moment hostilities resume. A peace is unstable unless its terms are perceived as just.

Peace is valuable not only as a way to escape the fears and worries of "the precincts of battalle." Peace makes possible enormous improvements in the material conditions of life. The soloist is willing to consider society itself as a cooperative venture for mutual advantage, to continue from generation to generation. From this viewpoint, she asks what fundamental rules would make this venture into a "good game," one that people will willingly play despite having no real choice. This, she realizes, is the closest it is practically possible to approach the ideal of government by consent.

Viewing society as this kind of venture, the soloist expects the social contract to address two issues. The first is, what basic rights do participants enjoy? The second is, by what principles are the benefits made possible by the venture to be distributed? Even someone who denies that there are any such rights or principles can agree that if a social contract were possible, it would address these two essential questions: what are my liberties, and what is my due?

A method is implicit in the way the investigation has gone. We start with an initial situation, or "original position," and ask, what rules would we agree to – if any! – were we to put aside what we know about our actual social position? This helps prevent our framing rules biased in our favor. We do this not only because biased rules are unfair, but also because biased rules are ones that others (who are not identically biased) can reasonably reject. The goal of the social contract is to secure a durable peace among people who do not share the same ultimate aims, or beliefs, or skin tone, or gender, or talents. The question thus has to be approached behind what John Rawls called "a veil of ignorance."

This is what we have had the soloist do in the preceding chapters. A basic equal right to freedom of conscience emerged. So also, a basic equal right to bodily integrity. A basic, equal right to choose one's associates and occupation. A basic equal right to own personal possessions. The soloist will insist on a social minimum, or social safety net: it would be unreasonable to expect others to honor a social contract that made no provision for spreading the individual's risk of injury, illness, and financial distress. This is far from socialism – a capitalist welfare state provides the same guarantee, even as it insists upon private ownership of the means of production.

As for other property rights, the soloist acknowledges that material inequality might be the precondition for greater material prosperity for everyone, or for the average person. She would not, however, sacrifice her basic equal rights for a shot at greater material wealth. That said, she also recognizes that equal liberty, in conditions of material economic inequality, makes it almost certain that the worth of the basic equal liberties will not be equal for all. A principle of equality governs the possession of the basic liberties, but a principle of responsibility governs the *worth* of the equal basic liberties. It is unlikely that any numerical ratio could be agreed to as a cap to the allowable degree of inequality of the worth of the equal basic liberties.

The political liberties have a special place among the equal basic liberties. The other liberties are such that their greater worth in the hands of some will normally, through the operation of enterprises in a market economy, bring about a greater worth – in absolute terms – for all. This is not the case for the political liberties: given the rivalrous nature of politics, greater political influence enjoyed by the materially better off will not lead to more affordable political influence enjoyed by the less well-off.

This is disturbing because, in the absence of any plausible principled cap to the relative degree of material inequality, the soloist looks to the democratic political process itself as a check on excessive accumulations of private wealth and social inequality. Such a check is necessary, indeed *critical*, to assure even a semblance of tolerably fair equality of opportunity from generation to generation. The well-off can be counted upon to favor their offspring regardless of whether the offspring are talented or not. If the well-off are free to employ their greater wealth in politics in service of this understandable favoritism, no assurance of social stability can be credible.

The soloist is drawn to the proposition that the "fair value," that is, the roughly equal worth, of the political liberties has to be credibly guaranteed by the social contract, over and above their formal equality. How this guarantee might be realized is the subject of the second half of the book. The principles enunciated in the first half are not acceptable in the role of a social contract unless they can be institutionalized and depended upon in practice.

Part Two

Getting Justice Done

5

Why Worry about "the Means of Production"?

A soloist will insist on having an equal say in shaping the institutions of the basic structure of society, within the bounds set by the equal basic rights. But the soloist insists that she have an *effectively* equal say. Those with greater wealth cannot dictate the political agenda, otherwise her consent to government cannot be counted on. Without an institutional structure that assures political equality, equality of opportunity cannot be expected. The wealthier would use their disproportionate influence in politics in favor of policies that privilege their offspring over others. The wealthier could also be suspected of using their greater political influence to tilt the economic playing field to favor their already favored situation.

We arrive at the question, what kinds of institutions are capable of realizing a social contract specified by the principles derived in Part One? In particular, what kinds of property rights will be institutionalized, and who will have them? We immediately perceive that slavery, that is, property in persons, will not feature in any social contract to which slaves could be counted on to adhere. We also immediately perceive that no social contract would allow people's organs to be taken without their specific, freely given consent.

Property in land is a late-arriving institution, in the long view of human history. Humans everywhere were hunter-gatherers until about forty thousand years ago. We humans lived in groups and bands that rarely numbered more than a few score. We had no fixed settlements, and often fought rival bands over access to good hunting and picking. The boundaries of these territories were unmarked and constantly in flux. The prey taken in the hunt and the nuts and berries gathered were shared.

With the advent of agriculture in the Indus Valley in the Middle East, we can discern the beginning of property as we know it today. The primitive communism of the hunter-gatherers gave way to the metes-and-bounds demanded by efficient agriculture. Jean-Jacques Rousseau described this epochal development this way: "The first person who, having enclosed a plot of ground, bethought himself to say this is mine, and found people simple enough to believe him, was the true founder of civil society" (Rousseau 1755: I, II, 1). A soloist would not like to be called "simple." She would not unthinkingly accept the encloser's audacious claim.

The soloist can see two sides to the story. Her own natural liberty has been curtailed. Whereas formerly she could roam and gather wherever she pleased, she now can do so only by the grace of someone else. How is this not theft? Part of philosopher John Locke's answer to this question was that the encloser who has improved her little plot, and not let the produce grown on it go to rot, "hath increased the common stock of mankind," and thus cannot be called a thief. By using money, humans have made it possible for the encloser to exchange the surplus of her harvest for something imperishable, silver or gold, that cannot go to spoil. So, Locke says, anyone who gets, spends, or otherwise uses money has thereby given her consent to a term of the social contract that approves, even sanctifies, the unequal accumulation of private property.

What Locke leaves out is the bit about how the enclosers – the landowners – managed to improve the output of the plots they enclosed. It was not by their labor alone, but by the labor of the landless, who were, in England, over centuries, gradually excluded from the commons as it was enclosed. The commoners became tenants. The reward they received for their labor barely sufficed for their needs, and the money gained in the market by the sale of the surplus went into the pockets of the landowning class. Why did the laborers not simply walk away and find their own land? Well, they did, once the legal bondage of feudalism was relieved, and the supposedly unsettled North American continent beckoned (we will come back to this later).

The idea that improvement of the common stock of mankind was a good and sufficient reason to limit liberty was an infectious one. Property, by definition, limits the liberty of those who do not own it. Your ownership of that plot of land you choose to call Blackacre consists in your right to call upon the public power to exclude me from it. Without that right, you would not bother as much to improve Blackacre, by irrigating it, tilling it, planting it with crops, and so on. The market distributes the added stock so others may benefit from your trouble.

The same rationale was easy to transfer to other kinds of improvement. Inventions and literary works improve the lot of mankind. It is absurd to think that, in a state of nature, the first human to use a slice of tree-trunk as a wheel thereby magically gained the exclusive moral right to barter tree-trunk slices for use as wheels. Likewise, it is absurd to think that the first human to whistle a happy tune somehow magically gained a moral right to be paid by others for the privilege of whistling that happy tune.

Even so, a lawmaker might reasonably calculate that if authors and inventors were given exclusive rights to "intellectual property," then the common stock of the nation and humankind would increase. My liberty to whistle that happy tune would be curtailed, but the institution would incentivize the creation of many more happy tunes.

The social contract does not exist for the benefit of some metaphysical organic entity called society. It exists for the benefit of individual people who are parties to it. They are conceived as having sacrificed their natural liberty in exchange for something more valuable, namely, the liberty of a citizen. The greater wealth that civil society produces is valuable because individual people benefit from it. It is not thought valuable because it is offered as a tribute to the great god, Society.

Vastly greater wealth is possible where people cooperate as if carrying out the terms of a social contract. The point of the contract is to secure peace and thereby to unleash the productive potential latent in individuals. The goal is to get that wealth into individual hands. How? And how are shares to be determined?

Thomas Hobbes, the sharpest and most notorious social-contract thinker, had some interesting things to say on the subject of property. He wrote, "at the entrance into conditions of Peace, no man [shall] require to reserve to himself any Right, which he is not content should be reserved to every one of the rest" (Hobbes 1651: 77). This is squared with everyone's retaining certain liberties, such "as a right to governe theire own bodies; enjoy aire, water, motion, waies to go from place to place; and all things else, without which a man cannot live, or not live well" (77). These liberties are, if you like, *inalienable*, for the same reason Hobbes gives for saying that one cannot be interpreted to have alienated one's right to resist the hangman. They are necessary to one's self-preservation.

Hobbes concedes that each of us has an equal right to exclusive property in our bodies, but which we only acquire upon entering civil society. In a condition of "meere nature," we have a right to whatever we think we need, even the bodies of others. Peace is impossible. His notorious solution is for everyone to surrender their natural liberty and merge into a Leviathan, an "artificiall man," who then appoints a sovereign to wield the common power, owing nothing to the people.

Hobbes *advises* (only God could *command*) the sovereign to divide the common wealth according to this rule: "*That such things as cannot be divided, be enjoyed in Common, if it can be; and if the quantity of the thing permit, without Stint; otherwise Proportionably* ... For otherwise the distribution is Unequall, and contrary to Equitie" (77). Hobbes cites "the common use of wells, ways, rivers, sacred things, &c." (1642: ch. IV, 14). He goes on to say "[For those things that] can neither be divided, nor enjoyed in common ... *That the Entire Right; or else, (making the use alternate,) the First Possession, be determined by Lot* ... and in some cases to the First-Borne..." (1651: 78). End of discussion. The soloist gathers from this a division of things into the following kinds:

Things that can be enjoyed in common, and things that cannot be enjoyed in common.

Things that can be divided, and things that cannot be divided.

And consequently there is the category of

Things that can neither be divided *nor* enjoyed in common.

As to this third, compound category, Hobbes says the ownership rule ought to be first-possession, or by lots, or, in certain unspecified cases, to the first-born. Whichever way, Hobbes allows there to be private property of things within the category of those things that can neither be divided nor enjoyed in common.

Land is something that can be divided and can also be enjoyed in common. The division of land into exclusive plots was the beginning of civil society, Rousseau said. Land divided is more productive, in most circumstances, than land held in common, in which all members of a group have a non-exclusive right to use and enjoy every part and its fruits. With new (to them) worlds still being discovered on Earth, Anglo-European minds could fancy an eventual day in which everybody might be a king in his own tiny kingdom.

The onset of an Industrial Revolution in the nineteenth century exploded this fantasy, overturning all former methods of production and the social relations they defined. It began with complicated apparatuses coming into use in large textile workshops like the Gobelins manufactory in France. What was new and different about these facilities was that they displaced cottage industry and could not be replicated at a smaller, household scale. A hand loom or a spinning wheel might fit into someone's parlor, but a waterwheel-powered broad loom fitted with a Jacquard patterning device could not.

Making free use of the energy density of fossil fuels, industries abruptly accelerated their exploitation of the possibilities of size and complexity. The Industrial Revolution was a world-historical event. In came big complicated machines that took many workers and specialists to operate, producing an output far greater than and often other than what those engaged in its production would need or care to consume.

Production was not meant for immediate consumption, but for sale in the market. The laborer's reward was not his product but his wage. Only recently freed from their ties to feudal estates, the "masterless men" of the English Midlands found themselves bound to wage-service in the "dark Satanic mills" depicted by poet William Blake. Private ownership of the mills and big machinery led inexorably to the laboring men's assignment to a class of propertyless laborers.

Private property and individual (white male) liberty were still reconcilable in the opinion of a host of enlightened optimists, including Tom Paine, Thomas Jefferson, and Abraham Lincoln, so long as the American frontier was open, where the possibility of independence from the masters still beckoned. Yet the frontier itself was accessible and productive to occupy only by grace of the railroad. Anyone could aspire to own 40 acres and a mule, but not everyone could own a system of railroads.

This was not a mere matter of affordability. Although

public lands might be parceled out to individuals as theirs to own separately, a railroad right-of-way could not. Network effects and returns to scale began to emerge, which put paid to any realistic dream that each yeoman might someday possess his own sovereign (if tiny) kingdom.

Hobbes had been the first to notice that there is a category of things that cannot practically be enjoyed in common or divided into individual parcels. As the Industrial Revolution turned the human world upside down, certain things emerged within this category that are practically necessary for making a living in a wage economy. These things have come to be called "the means of production."

The core idea is this: *the means of production* in a given society, at a given time, consist of those resources and instrumentalities that have two characteristics:

1. they are widely indispensable means of productive activity (or their products are); and
2. they are impossible to be severally owned.

"Several ownership" means practicable ownership – especially the right to exclusive use and enjoyment – by each and every person, individually. A shovel does not belong among the means of production, because it is easily possible for everyone to own – that is, to have by right the exclusive use of – his or her own shovel, and the utility (or "use-value") of owning a shovel is not diminished by everyone's owning one.

A highway system, on the other hand, does belong to the means of production. A single person or group might own the highway system, but several ownership of the highway system is absurd. If everyone owned his or her own stretch of highway, there would be no highway system. Unlike shovels, the utility of highways depends on their forming a more-or-less continuous network.

Similarly, units of a currency may be severally owned, but the currency itself belongs to the means of production.

We cannot each of us issue a currency. Of course, we can give out coupons and chits and occasional IOUs – but this is a far cry from the kind of common currency that makes commerce possible. Public ownership of the currency is possible. Monopoly or oligopoly ownership of currencies is possible. But several ownership of a currency is not.

It is easy to confuse several ownership with some other kinds of ownership. They are not the same.

Common ownership is a different concept from several ownership. Several owners have the right to exclude others from their several parcels; common owners do not have the right to exclude others from the commons. Hence there is a risk of "tragic" overuse of a commons. If you and I each own a herd of cattle, the pastureland held in common could be over-grazed. Nothing, yet, stops either of us from letting our herds eat freely.

Share ownership is a different concept from several ownership. Corporate shareholders have rights to a share of whatever dividends the directors choose to distribute; and, typically, shareholders have voting rights. Shareholders typically do not have a right to a several parcel of the corporation's assets (except upon its liquidation, if anything is left after the prior claims of its creditors are satisfied). Normally, a mere shareholder has no more right to access, use, or enjoy the corporation's assets than a non-shareholding member of the public has.

That clarifies what several ownership is and is not. Now, more about the means of production. These belong to Hobbes's category of things that can neither be usefully owned in common nor divided into parts or parcels that everyone could own one (or more) of. The defining addition to Hobbes's category is that access to the means of production is essential to living a productive life in the economy as it exists.

The soloist will want to compare this idea with concepts she may have been exposed to in ECON 101.

"Natural" monopoly is a different concept from the means of production. A natural monopoly exists where a

single actor can satisfy a market for a good or service more efficiently than multiple actors can. Competition would be inefficient. The definition of the means of production is simpler: it makes no reference to efficiencies, the presence and degree of which will depend on the slope of marginal and average cost curves, as empirically determined by the market to be served, returns to scale, costs of entry, and so on.

The extension of "the means of production" will not include natural monopolies for luxury items, and it may well include things that are not natural monopolies. Automaking is not a natural monopoly, but auto factories are among the means of production, though not the autos themselves. It would be absurdly inefficient for everyone to make his or her own cars, but not necessarily inefficient at all for there to be multiple car makers. And, where I come from, a car is a necessity (although, under socialism, it could cease to be).

"*Public goods*" are a different concept from the means of production. A public good is any commodity (whether or not put to use productively) as to which consumption is non-exclusive and non-rivalrous. The classic example is national defense. My being protected from foreign invasion is not diminished by your being equivalently protected; and I cannot practically be excluded from the good of national security once it is provided.

There is possible overlap between the means of production and the category of public goods: the military is an example. But the overlap is imperfect. Means of production like a highway system are not a public good in the strictest sense. Access can be, and is, restricted, and consumption is not non-rivalrous (quite the contrary, where I live).

I say "widely indispensable means of productive activity" to sidestep the issue of highly specialized productive needs. A Stradivarius might be an indispensable means to productive activity as a concert violinist at the highest international level; and several ownership is not practically possible. I insert "widely" to bring about the intuitively correct result that a Stradivarius would not count among the means of production. Violins of lesser renown can be severally owned, so they do not count either.

There is no certainty that there will be anything answering to these criteria in every place and era. In primitive or hand-to-mouth circumstances, there might only be simple tools that can only be manipulated by a single handler. Rousseau wrote a speculative history of technology, leading from "natural weapons, branches and stones," to the invention of "line and hook," "bows and arrows," and the use of "traps," "skins," and "fire." In this progression, "the means of production" do not yet exist.

Looking ahead from where we stand now in history, we can fancy that on some not-too-distant future day every person will own his or her very own personal, self-assembling, self-maintaining, solar-powered 3D printer that converts air into food, clothing, housing, transportation, entertainment, and whatever you will. The means of production, as defined here, would no longer exist.

Set these extremes aside. Now and around here, the means of production include the currency, the highway system, the postal service, the broadcast spectrum, telecommunications, power generation and distribution, navigable waterways, credit, investment banking, insurance, weaponry and munitions, airways, railways, hospitals, agribusiness, many extractive industries, petrochemicals, internet service providers, Facebook, Amazon (especially Amazon Web Services), Google, and so forth.

We can imagine everyone having a share (equal or unequal) of the revenues of such things, and we can imagine everyone having a say (equal or unequal) in the overall direction of such things. But we cannot imagine dividing such things into separate, exclusive parcels. If we imagine distributing these things to each, we find that we will have hugely and even radically diminished the whole. We can imagine everyone self-insuring, for example, but that amounts to imagining that the institution of insurance no longer exists at all.

The key thing is not bigness. Not everything that happens to be a big business that supplies something that is meant to enable people to engage in productive activity is included in the means of production. Coca-Cola and the caffeinated beverage industry to which it belongs are big business, but are not among the means of production – except possibly on a local scale, as might be the case in a small town in which the soda-bottling plant is the major employer.

Something might belong to the means of production on a wide scale, but it does not follow that every local or small-scale part does. A farmer's shovel or tractor does not belong to the means of production merely because the farmer's small operation is functionally integrated into larger operations that can properly be called agribusiness. Often, and especially now, the means of production are platforms or networks. The nodes might be severally owned, but often there are central facilities that the nodes have to rely on, and which cannot be severally owned.

Think of the gigantic grain elevators scattered along the railway spurs on the Great Plains of North America. If ten severally owned farms are served by one massive elevator, each farm might be allotted its own silo. But it would be impracticable for each silo to be assigned its own rail link, its own access road, and so forth.

The information age has taken us beyond the Industrial Revolution in significant ways. Control of a platform conveys with it enormous power over those who need to use it to engage in productive activity or to market what they produce.

Apple's App Store is one example. As a condition for the privilege of marketing the apps they design for the iOS operating system, developers must agree to let Apple make the app obsolete by Apple's copying it and incorporating the copy into iOS. A single device is not part of the means of production, on my analysis, but the platform it runs on could be, and in the case of iOS, it is.

Wherever there is something answering to the description "the means of production" – i.e., widely indispensable means to productive life that cannot be severally owned – social relations are altered by that very fact; and now there is an additional, distinctive danger of domination and subordination. The promise that with hard work everyone can aspire to be an independent sovereign in her very own domain, is delusory.

The soloist recalls her AMERICAN CIV 101. Abraham Lincoln was a keen observer of the direction the United States was taking as a result of the Industrial Revolution. The founding generation had pictured a commercial but primarily agricultural society. Lincoln, no less than Jefferson, believed that it was "in the nature of things" that farmers would comprise the majority of voters. With westward expansion, yeoman farmers and their families were expected to form the typical units of society: independent, but governed locally and democratically for the most part.

The American Civil War was precipitated by a dispute within the white citizenry over the extension of slavery into the western territories seeking admission to the Union. The subtext of a speech Lincoln gave in 1859 at the Wisconsin Agricultural Society Fair was that not only slavery but also industrialization was a threat to liberty and democratic government. What he said was of urgent importance to the "masterless men" of the American Midwest, as they anticipated the insinuation of new means of production into agriculture. Would this make farmers more dependent than they already were on those money-kings called banks?

Pressure to allow slavery derived in part from the circumstance that free labor was in short supply in the territories. Lincoln was struck by a study showing that, nationally, the potential productivity of land, in terms of bushels of wheat and corn, was far higher than its average realized product. He argued that the key to increasing output lay in what he called "*thorough* cultivation," that is, the application of new methods and devices to the soil.

The great question was, how was this to be done? Lincoln wrote:

> The world is agreed that *labor* is the source from which human wants are mainly supplied. There is no dispute upon this point. From this point, however, men immediately diverge. Much disputation is maintained as to the best way of applying and controlling the labor element. By some it is assumed that labor is available only in connection with capital – that nobody labors, unless somebody else, owning capital, somehow, by the use of that capital, induces him to do it ... [T]hey naturally conclude that all laborers are necessarily either *hired* laborers, or *slaves*. They further assume that whoever is once a hired laborer, is fatally fixed in that condition for life; and thence again that his condition is as bad as, or worse than that of a slave. This is the *"mud-sill"* theory. (Lincoln 1953: III, 477–8)

Lincoln did not use the word *proletarians* to designate this permanent army of wage-slaves forming society's mud-sill, fated to bear the foot traffic of progress. In America, ironically, the sharpest critiques of emerging industrial capitalism issued from the pens and tongues of apologists for chattel slavery. Mud-sill thinking could be turned to the advantage of those seeking to expand slavery into the western territories. Ducking the race issue, Lincoln's reply to mud-sill-ism hints at a social contract between free equals, meant to include proletarian hirelings as well as masterless men, capitalists, and landowners.

He begins by sketching an opposing theory, *"free* labor," which he takes his audience already to favor. According to this theory, one error of the mud-sill theory is to ignore the fact that the great majority

> neither work for others, nor have others working for them ... are neither slaves nor masters ... are neither *hirers* nor *hired*. Men, with their families – wives, sons and daughters

– work for themselves, on their farms, in their houses and
in their shops, taking the whole product to themselves, and
asking no favors of capital on one hand, nor of hirelings or
slaves on the other. (1953: III, 478)

The free-labor theory declares that the interest of the
political majority of the nation is not vested in the existence
of a permanent underclass as its mud-sill. Evidence?

There is a demonstration for saying this. Many independent
men, in this assembly, doubtless a few years ago were
hired laborers. And their case is almost if not quite the
general rule. (1953: III, 478)

If there were any in Lincoln's audience who were exceptions to this general rule, they would not have been likely
to sing out an objection. Lincoln knows they are present,
and now speaks to them:

The prudent, penniless beginner in the world, labors for
wages awhile, saves a surplus with which to buy tools or
land, for himself; then labors on his own account another
while, and at length hires a new beginner to help him.
(1953: III, 478–9)

Several ownership of tools and land is the necessary key
to taking the big step up from hireling to yeoman, and
is necessary to the working of this "just and prosperous
system." Necessary, but not necessarily sufficient.
Free-labor theory explains:

If any continue through life in the condition of the hired
laborer, it is not the fault of the system, but because of
either a dependent nature which prefers it, or improvi-
dence, folly, or singular misfortune. (1953: III, 479)

Unequal outcomes are not the fault of the system that
offers a path to independence to all who care to take

it. Pursued diligently, the path will normally allow the hireling to attain equal membership among his peers in the politically powerful "middle" class.

Lincoln cautions that prudence and diligence will not suffice if education is lacking. The future belongs to *thorough* work in agriculture, competence in which demands knowledge and skills that the mere hireling can do without – skills which, in fact, the capitalist would prefer that the hireling not have. From the mud-sill theory's perspective, educated proletarian heads "are regarded as explosive materials," on a par with the heads of educated slaves.

Recall that the free-labor theory – more aptly called, the *ladder* theory – relies on several ownership of tools and land as the instrument making social advancement possible. Several ownership, as I defined it earlier in this chapter, is practicable ownership, by each. Tools can be severally owned. Land can be severally owned, but the burning question was whether land can be productive if it is held in parcels small enough to be independently worked.

If only larger acreages were practical to own, then where was the labor going to come from? The mud-sill argument was that it came down to a choice between white wage-slaves and African outright-slaves – slavery either way. Lincoln could not let that stand.

So, much of his speech was concerned with the prospects of a "steam plow," which could solve the riddle. Independent, self-educated men could apply the enormous potential of steam power to the problem of bringing out the productive potential of land – on parcels small enough for yeoman families to own and manage, and without having to rely on hirelings or slaves. Once perfected, affordably manufactured, and severally owned, the steam plow would stand as the refutation of mud-sill, and the vindication of the free-soil opposition to extending slavery into the territories. *Thorough* cultivation – mechanized agriculture – excluded wage slavery and chattel slavery alike.

Lincoln concludes his case with a forecast of the future course of the nation:

> Population must increase rapidly – more rapidly than in former times – and ere long the most valuable of arts, will be the art of deriving a comfortable subsistence from the smallest area of soil [– "*thorough* work"]. No community whose every member possesses this art, can ever be the victim of oppression in any of its forms. Such community will be alike independent of crowned-kings, money-kings, and land-kings. (1953: III, 481)

Lincoln anticipates that the steam plow, when it comes to be perfected, will be available to "every member." He dismissed the possibility that the steam plow would not be available to the smallholding farmer. He expressed no fear that mechanized agriculture would lead to agribusiness. His fixed opinion was that thorough cultivation was small-scale cultivation: "Mammoth farms are like tools or weapons, which are too heavy to be handled. Ere long they are thrown aside, at a great loss" (1953: III, 476).

In this vision, westward expansion would be achieved by citizen-farmers whose educated skill at thorough cultivation would assure their independence of the money-kings. Lincoln did not ask whether it would keep them independent, too, of the coming *railroad*-kings.

Each diligent hireling could hope someday to become a free-holding agriculturist, and each prudent farmer might hope one day to operate his own steam plow. The greater wealth of the land-kings and the money-kings could not faze the indomitable American soloist, in his pursuit of happiness through *thorough* cultivation.

The Civil War interrupted the unfolding of Lincoln's vision. A greatly hastened westward expansion was needed to outflank the Confederacy. There was federal public land in abundance between Omaha and the Pacific. Homesteaders could be lured westward by the promise of free land, if only there were railroads to get them there and to transport what they produced to market. How to finance a transcontinental railroad?

Railroad financing was a subject Lincoln had a longstanding interest in. In his early career, he found the cost of building a railroad spur in Illinois daunting (1953: I, 5–6). As a candidate for the U.S. Congress, he advocated selling federal lands and granting the proceeds to the states, to enable them to build railroads without having to borrow and pay interest on debt (1953: I, 48). In the Illinois legislature, he co-sponsored a bill to incentivize private enterprise by guaranteeing a 6 percent return, but with the state holding an option to buy the completed railroad for a sum computed on that basis (1953: 54, 251).

The Pacific Railroad Act of 1862 involved a breathtaking gift of public land to private corporate interests. The Railroad and Homestead Acts, together, eventually ceded an area of public land equivalent in size to the states of Texas and California, combined. Lincoln defended the giveaway in these terms:

> It has long been a cherished opinion of some of our wisest statesmen that the people of the United States had a higher and more enduring interest in the early settlement and substantial cultivation of the public lands than in the amount of direct revenue to be derived from the sale of them. This opinion has had a controlling influence in shaping legislation upon the subject of our national domain. I may cite, as evidence of this … the *grants* to railway companies of alternate sections of land upon the contemplated lines of the roads which, when completed, will so largely multiply the facilities for reaching our distant possessions. (1953: VII, 46–7; annual address to Congress, December 8, 1863; my emphasis).

The grant included not merely the checkerboard of adjacent land, and the right-of-way, but also ownership of the railroad itself. The United States retained no option to buy.

The involvement of the money-kings of that time in persuading a wartime Congress to crown the railroad-kings is a story that will not be investigated here. Neither will the further adventures of the railroad-kings – also known as "the Robber Barons" – be retold here. It is enough for the soloist's information to note that Lincoln's assurance of continuing and ever greater independence, which he gave the Wisconsin agriculturists in 1859, could not stand in the wake of the great giveaway of 1862. Every hireling and yeoman farmer might aspire to someday own a steam plow – but he could not aspire to own a railroad.

A railroad is a paradigm instance of the means of production. Compare a railroad to an equivalent area of pastureland. Tenancy in common is possible on pastureland. If one of your sheep bumps into one of mine, it's not a catastrophe. Tenancy in common of a rail line is different. If your locomotive bumps into mine, that could easily be a catastrophe. A pasture can be divided into smaller parcels that are still usable – perhaps even more usable. A railroad cannot be divided into parcels that have much if any use in individual hands. It is the railroad as a network that has utility. A network that each and every one may use as she pleases is chaos, and a network that is sliced into individually owned segments is next to useless.

Crucially, the network is essential to thorough culti-vation. The railroad became the means of production in nineteenth-century America. Its private owners quickly came to dominate the political life of every state and locality, and of the nation itself. Private ownership of the means of production threatened to fuse farmers, hirelings, and freedmen alike into a permanent mud-sill class.

The soloist can appreciate that this is a case in which unequal wealth strangled political equality. What is to prevent that happening whenever there are the means of production and they are privately held? The question is especially apt today, in this age of the information-kings.

6

Making Political Equality Real

The soloist's need to spell out how the terms of a social contract can be realized in practice forces her now to attend to institutional possibilities.

We hope to arrange political institutions in such a way that everyone can accept the pattern of economic inequalities, whatever it happens to be, the same way poker players accept a final distribution of chips, whatever it turns out to be. This hope depends, though, on the political process assuring that all concerned have an equal say.

How is it possible to assure that everyone has an equal say if some are able to use their greater wealth to influence the political process? Political equality, to be real, has to mean not merely formal, one-person/one-vote equality. That would be consistent with letting the wealthier decide what is put to a vote (and what isn't) and influence what laws are carried out (and which ones are mere dead-letters).

The soloist would not consent to a social contract drawn up in a way that allowed that to happen, if there were an alternative. This is why the practical question of how to make political equality a reality, rather than mere rhetoric, is urgent. Is there any alternative to allowing unequal wealth gradually to dominate the political process? As Rousseau said, "when a Giant and a Dwarf travel the same road, every step they take will give the Giant an added advantage" (1755: II, I, 47). And it matters not a whit if the dwarves are in the majority.

There are two basic approaches to the problem of money in politics. One is to impose a limit on the ways money gets moved around and spent. The other is to impose a limit of some sort on the degree to which wealth itself is allowed to accumulate in private hands.

Before going into the question of which approach is better (maybe they can be mixed), the soloist will notice that something has to be done at the threshold, before the ordinary political and legislative processes get started – in fact, before those processes are set up.

The social contract serves as the constitution of a political society. In many countries it is commonplace to think of a constitution as a written document, effective on such-and-such a date, enacted with conspicuous ceremonial formalities. The constitution is more than a sheet of parchment or vellum, however, and more than the words that compose it. The constitution includes the common understandings and norms that surround the document itself – if there is any document at all. The British constitution is still largely unwritten. That, and all other constitutions possess whatever power and legitimacy they have in virtue of the shared political culture that gives rise to and sustains them.

Every political constitution sets up a process by which laws are to be made. Typically, the process is exclusive of other ways of making law. Also typically, this legislative process is a majoritarian one. The processes the soloist is interested in are democratic ones. In a polity of any considerable size, legislative power will be vested in a representative assembly.

A fundamental element of the social contract is a settlement about what is and is not a proper subject matter for majoritarian decision. The equal basic rights, for example, are not subject to limitation by a majority vote. Liberty of conscience means, at the least, that the majority may not, by ordinary legislation, impose a uniform religious practice on everybody.

Similarly, the constitution includes certain ground rules governing the conduct of the political process that the ordinary legislative process cannot alter by itself. The principle of one-person/one-vote, for example, is essential to any social contract that the soloist could commit to. The U.S. Constitution – the document – does not state this principle in so many words. Only after dogged litigation did the U.S. Supreme Court recognize that one-person/one-vote is demanded by the constitution, in the "higher law" sense, and thus must govern how the documentary constitution is to be interpreted.

The crucial matter for the soloist is that her substantive political equality be assured by the design of the democratic process, and by the support it draws from the wider political culture. The soloist will not accept the assurance that, in any event, political majorities will always, or eventually, do the right thing. No social contract that can command her rational assent can fail to commit to whatever it takes to assure the equal worth of her formally equal political liberties. One-person/one-vote is not enough. The social contract must provide that she has as much a role as anyone else, equally ready and able, in setting the agenda that is to be discussed and voted on. It must also provide that she has much a right as anyone else, equally ready and able, to insist upon the rule of law.

So, the design of measures needed to assure the equal worth of political liberty cannot be left to ordinary legislative action. This design has to cabin and direct the legislative process. The justice of legislation is mainly a matter of whether the law is an outcome of a process that respects and reflects the political equality of all who are expected to think of themselves as consenting to it as its authors.

What are the devices that the social contract can put to work?

The first type of device comprises *insulation* devices. In conditions of economic inequality, the greater wealth of some can be kept out of the political process altogether, or regulated, or minimized. Of course, some money is always and necessarily going to be part of a political process. Ballots have to be printed, ballot-boxes have to be built, someone has to count and announce the results. This is a bare minimum. A vigorous democratic process will involve discussion and debate, which means assembly halls, media publicity and coverage, and so on. A representative democracy will provide opportunities for constituents to meet and to try to influence their representatives. And so on.

Insulation devices are meant to control the entry of money into politics. They can be designed in ways that not only limit the amount, but also assure that those with more money to spend gain no advantage. They can, for example, fund debates exclusively from public money, or even subsidize parties. The flip side of subsidies consists of caps. Caps can be imposed on either the spending side or the contribution side, or on both.

Insulation devices are attractive because they are focused and not too ambitious. They focus on the problem of maintaining political equality and they address that problem and nothing else. If economic inequality overall is too great (or not great enough), the diagnosis and the remedy are matters for legislative deliberation and action in a representative democracy under majority rule.

The second type of device could be called the *anti-accumulation* devices. The idea here is to prevent and if necessary to break up private holdings of wealth, so that the pattern of holdings is never dangerously unequal. One example is an inheritance tax or estate tax – also known by the pejorative term, "death tax." The aim is to limit inter-generational transmission of wealth. One thought is that, since no one deserves to be born to wealthy parents, the inheritor has less of an equitable claim to what amounts to a windfall. Another thought is that the prospect of receiving an inheritance creates a perverse incentive to be less productive.

Another example of an anti-accumulation device is a constitutional ban on certain forms of ownership. For instance, a ban on slavery means that no one can accumulate property in that form. No class of wealthy slaveholders would exist, and hence the political equality of non-slaveholders – to say nothing of slaves – would to that extent not be threatened.

Similarly, a constitutional ban on private ownership of the means of production would mean that no private person or class could accumulate property in that form. Hence, the political equality of non-owners of the means of production would to that extent not be jeopardized.

Antitrust laws are another example of an anti-accumulation device. One thought behind them is that private monopolists in a market have no incentive to increase output. The monopolist is indifferent between making money by supplying less while charging more and supplying more while charging less. In a competitive market, all producers in the market have an incentive to charge less and produce more, which benefits consumers. A different thought is that society benefits when small producers thrive, even if that means higher prices for consumers than would be the case if larger producers were permitted to drive smaller ones out of business. Although the immediate purpose of antitrust laws, and estate taxes, may not be to protect the political process, they can serve that end indirectly.

Instances of these two types of device – *insulation* and *anti-accumulation* – can also be mixed. The questions for the soloist are: Which devices are capable of being installed as constitutional guarantees? And are they, alone or in some combination, adequate to the task?

Insulation devices are fairly common. Bribery of officials is a defined criminal offense in every country I know of. Bribery is indirectly forbidden in the U.S. Constitution, which makes "treason, bribery, and other high crimes and misdemeanors" a ground for removing an officer. Obviously, the wealthy have greater means and more opportunities to bribe officials – possibly greater reason to, also – and so criminalizing bribery is a step in the direction of defending political equality.

Only a small step, however. The U.S. Supreme Court has upheld federal campaign statutory law that caps individual contributions to individual candidates. But it has invalidated statutory limits on individual or corporate contributions to political causes, so long as they are not coordinated with a candidate's campaign. Moreover, the Court has invalidated statutory limits on campaign *spending* altogether. (Media mogul Michael Bloomberg lavished one of his billions in a futile four-month campaign for the 2020 *Democratic* Party nomination – leaving him with a mere 59 billion dollars.) Political spending, in the Court's analysis, is political *speech*, and as such is entitled to the highest measure of protection against legal limitation.

Another type of insulation device assures a spending floor. This serves in effect to subsidize political discussion and parties and/or candidates. The relative advantage of the wealthier candidate and the candidate with wealthier friends is reduced. Publicly funded debates can give less well-known candidates a forum that supplements whatever they might be able to afford by way of paid advertising.

Spending floors and spending caps do not readily translate into satisfactory constitutional guarantees. The *effectiveness* – let's call it – of a constitutional guarantee varies as a function of the obviousness of its violations. The most effective guarantees are those that are hardest to break without getting caught at it. The least effective guarantees are ones whose, say, vagueness, makes it hard for people to tell whether they are being honored or not, which in turn makes their legal enforcement more problematic.

A second dimension of the satisfactoriness of a constitutional guarantee is what we can call its *plausibility*:

the plausibility of a constitutional guarantee varies as a function of its non-arbitrariness. As illustrations of effectiveness and plausibility, consider the age qualifications for officeholders that are found in some constitutions.

The U.S. Constitution, for example, states that a member of the House of Representatives must be at least twenty-five years old, and have been a citizen for at least seven years. This provision is highly effective in the sense that the age and the length of citizenship of a person are readily determinable, objective facts. On the other hand, it is not a highly plausible provision. It is meant to guarantee that members are loyal and have good judgment. The numbers are proxies for qualities that are hard to determine, and their accuracy as proxies is doubtful. The specific numbers are arbitrary not only in the sense that they could have been otherwise: they are arbitrary in the sense that the case for using them as proxies at all seems weak. Moreover, it's not as though a line had to be drawn somewhere – there is no age qualification at all for judges, why need there be one for legislators?

A *satisfactory* constitutional guarantee, let's say, will score high in terms of both effectiveness and plausibility. Spending floors and caps are effective to the degree that they are quantitative rather than qualitative. By the same token, though, they seem to be less plausible, because the quantities chosen can seem arbitrary.

Quantitative terms, as a general matter, are the proper subjects of ordinary legislation. Trial and error is involved in getting them right, and changed circumstances can easily make them outdated, no longer high enough or low enough. For this reason, legislatures routinely delegate the job of setting quantitative standards to administrative agencies.

The point is easy to illustrate. Suppose there is a constitutional provision stating that an individual is allowed to donate no more than a certain $n to a political candidate. The value of $n can vary significantly over time. Inflation can lessen it, an increasing cost of media advertising can lessen it, the availability of social media can increase it. A number, n, adequate at one time may not be adequate at another. As a constitutional provision, though, it will be difficult for the popular majority to adjust the amount. Constitutional changes distinctively require supermajority support, and often have to get a supermajority at each of multiple stages of an amendment process.

Flexibility *can* be built into a constitutionalized numerical provision. Even so, in this instance, no non-arbitrary work-around is easy to come up with. Suppose the constitution were to specify the contribution cap at $\$n$, but were to define n as a percentage of per capita GDP. That would achieve a degree of flexibility but would simultaneously diminish both the effectiveness and the plausibility of the provision. What if GDP goes out of fashion or is discredited as lacking relevant significance? Whose heads go into the per capita? Per person? Per adult? Per employed person? Etc. Balancing all the relevant factors is grist for the legislative mill. What we seek, though, is a prior assurance of political equality, so that everyone can be confident that the balance, whatever the legislature determines, does not result from a prior, unfair tilt of the playing field.

We do not really expect to settle on numbers in the social contract, at least not beyond very simple equations like one person = one vote. Turning to the constitution as the blueprint for the structure of the government, the numbers we find and expect are still very simple: e.g., the number of branches of government, the number of chambers of the legislative branch, terms of years of offices, the minimum number of representatives per thousand residents, etc. If these numbers are arbitrary, they are typically so only in a fairly benign sense. They do make adjustment by ordinary legislation impossible, but that is precisely their point. Ordinary legislation follows processes defined within this structure.

Another instance of an insulation device aims at closing the "revolving door" between public service and private employment. Wherever the private sector can offer higher salaries than the government pays, officials are subject to a constant temptation. An official's expertise, experience, and connections could attract lucrative offers of private employment. It can reasonably be feared that an official who, say, regulates a certain industry, might regulate more lightly if she looks forward to moving over to a cushier job working for a firm in that industry.

Again, an anti-revolving-door provision is a poor candidate for an effective constitutional safeguard. The most effective such provision would impose a lifetime ban against leaving public service for any private-sector job. This would amount to creating a class of Mandarins, who might become civil servants by passing qualifying examinations given at a young age, and remain for life (somewhat as U.S. Supreme Court justices are apt to do) or until mandatory and comfortable retirement.

The acceptability of constitutionalizing an independent civil service is doubtful, anyway. A lifetime appointment conflicts with democratic accountability, which counts for something – quite a lot, in fact. Setting the length of terms of office need not be implausibly arbitrary. The problem is how are the out-of-a-job civil servants to make a living? Are they forbidden for life to work in sectors their former official service had touched on? That would rather discourage abler people from joining the civil service in the first place. Forbidden, then, only for a term of years? Fixing a time period for this, as a constitutional matter, seems less plausible.

But suppose there were some effective means of constitutionalizing an independent civil service; while that would keep private money out of the administration of government, it could not plausibly keep it out of the legislative and elective processes – unless the Mandarins were entrusted (like Plato's guardians) with lawmaking as well.

The soloist is repelled by the idea of submitting to the rule of incorruptible philosopher-kings. Even if she were sure she would be among them, she would not risk being overlooked. Anyway, her self-assurance is not so high that she would assume that those subjected to her guardianship would submit cheerfully.

A democratic idea that could assure political equality would be to fill offices at random, "sortition." Political power would rotate at regular intervals among officers chosen by lottery. What would be lost in expertise, experience, and possibly also in zeal, would be more than made up by a gain in assurances of political equality. This thought-bubble will not float far before bursting. Whatever sense rotating personnel randomly might make for administering the law fails to carry over easily to the matter of lawmaking. The lottery winners (so to speak) lack accountability, and since they know what position in private society they occupy, and will return to whatever they do, they may design laws for their own benefit.

To summarize, the insulation devices just surveyed do not appear to be fit candidates to make into constitutional fixtures. The soloist wants an assurance that her political equality is durable, and she wants to see this assurance not merely as writing on a sheet of parchment. She wants to see it built into the institutions that structure her life, however she chooses to live it.

She wants it built in so securely that she can accept being among the poorest class, knowing that she is the political equal of the richest. So also, if she happens to be among the richest class, she can embrace the restrictions on her spending as justified. The richest soloist will know that the willing cooperation of others in a system founded, ultimately, on threats of coercive force, will not be forthcoming unless they see themselves as her political equal.

Unfortunately, none of the insulation devices we just surveyed stand out as high scorers as to both effectiveness and plausibility. It remains a possibility that some combination of contribution caps, spending caps, subsidies, sortition, and inducements to independent civil service would score higher. The soloist begins to suspect, though, that stitching such elements together will likely only aggravate concerns that the guarantee of political equality is unsatisfactory, and especially so in times when the range of material inequality appears to be widening. Sometimes Sweden is pointed to as a model of how to insulate money from politics: yet the increasing degree of material inequality in that country over recent decades, fueled by tax breaks legislated for the rich, undermines confidence in the Swedish example (Johnson 2019). We will return to the case of Sweden later as an example of how the wealthy jealously guard their hold on the means of production.

So, the soloist turns to the other type of devices, the anti-accumulation devices.

One idea is to focus on intergenerational transfers. The most *effective* such device would simply ban inheritance altogether. At death, the wealth accumulated over the deceased's lifetime would simply "escheat" to the state. It would also be *plausible*, in the sense of its being non-arbitrary. Thus, as I've used these expressions, a "death duty" of 100 percent would be a *satisfactory* means to the end of curbing accumulation of wealth across generations. Obviously, it would also have to apply to gifts "*inter vivos*," lest the duty be avoided as the wealth-holder's death approached.

A 100 percent death duty, in itself, would still allow unlimited accumulation of wealth within a lifetime. The soloist sees this kind of accumulation as both inevitable, being the result of free exchanges, and as a desirable incentive to channel one's productive efforts to meet the needs of others. Besides, excesses could be addressed by income, property, and wealth taxation set at rates gauged to mitigate economic inequality.

At this point, one might interject a question: why not focus on income and wealth taxes on the living, rather than on intergenerational transfers? The answer to this is that tax rates and tax brackets are not *satisfactory* constitutional guarantees of political equality.

Tax rates and brackets are *effective*, in the sense that they can be defined with enough precision to allow

taxes owed to be calculated and underpayments objectively to be detected. Unfortunately, the more effective
a tax schedule is, the less *plausible* it becomes. The line-
drawing questions that have to be settled require arbitrary
decisions: how many brackets? Where are they set? What
marginal rates? Etc. Wherever they are set, the rationale
for setting them there rather than another place is unlikely
to answer doubts about the wisdom of giving them the
fixity that constitutional provisions distinctively possess.

There will indeed be good reasons to favor a presumption
that the tax schedule ought not to be tinkered with
frequently or at the behest of majority whim. Those
reasons, however, cannot ground a reasonable conviction
that the tax schedule, with its rates and brackets, does
exactly what it takes to assure political equality, just *nails*
it. By comparison, a 100% death duty is more plausible.
The death of a citizen is a salient event, and 100%
precisely matches the amount of wealth the deceased will
not be taking with her.

So, as between income taxes and estate taxes, the estate
tax appears to be the more plausible anti-accumulation
measure. Once the rate schedule begins to get complicated,
in order to make it more palatable, the constitutionalized
estate tax loses its advantage over income and wealth
taxes, in terms of plausibility. That is because the setting
of brackets and rates inevitably presents itself as requiring
revisable legislative judgment rather than a settled social
consensus.

But leaving the protection of political equality to the
judgment of political majorities already in power is like
closing the barn door after the cow has gotten out. It is
already too late.

If the *effectiveness* of estate taxation as a device to
protect political equality means outright confiscation at
death, the device would be too unpopular ever to make
its way into the social contract. *Plausibility* is diminished
by moving to a more complicated scheme of thresholds,
brackets, and rates; furthemore, the very idea of taxation

of estates is not as popular as one might suppose and hope. (Recall the popular appeal of the families-first principle.) A case can be made for imposing the tax on recipients rather than on the estate itself. That way, the owner can give it all away, but only by giving it widely.

Nevertheless, many people cling to the belief that a parent or grandparent ought to be able to transfer at least most of her wealth, intact, to her nearest and dearest. For many people, their life's project comes down to this: to boost their offspring and their offspring's offspring as high as they can in the social order.

Admittedly, this attitude is the product of conditioning, and it is possible that over time the popular ethos might reverse its polarity on the issue. The soloist would like to think of herself as "self-made," and to have lifted herself by her own bootstraps. She would like her children to be self-reliant and sturdy. Even so, she shivers at the very mention of a "death tax"; and, on reflection, she realizes that promising to change the popular ethos in this particular is not going to win the social contract many subscribers.

One of the many odd things about the human species is how long it takes for a newborn to become even minimally capable of looking out for itself. Consequently, human development requires an enormous investment of parental or other caregiver time and trouble – exceeding two decades-worth in many cases. People who have made or look forward to making this kind of investment are very likely to resent any attempt to reduce their identification with their offspring, in any way. Taxing inheritances hurts even more than taxing incomes, even though the legator is dead and gone before the taxman comes.

Estate taxation in some form and degree still ought to be a legislative option, whose exercise all can accept – if, but only if, the background conditions already establish political equality. If a liberal democracy already secures real political equality, then the legislature can be counted upon to impose taxes sufficient and necessary to assure that intergenerational transfers of wealth do not threaten to undermine political equality. On the other hand, if real political equality is not already and independently secured, then those with greater wealth can be expected to use that wealth as a means to clear away legal obstacles to their transmitting their wealth *entire* to their offspring.

Shouldn't parents be ashamed to use their greater wealth this way even if political equality is already secure? Anyway, how can political equality ever be secure until a social ethos has taken hold that shames those who use their advantages to influence the law to favor themselves and their families further? The soloist may recall Rousseau's remark about the social contract: the idea is to take people as they are and laws as they might be. The task is to state how the law might structure things so that people, as they are, and whatever their place in society, can see that their social system is basically just, and should be kept that way.

The grip of the idea that people have a right to do whatever they like with the property they fairly acquire is not absolute. Some forms of property have been abolished in modern history, and nobody mourns their going. Slavery is an example. Another is what lawyers call the "entail," an English form of ownership meant to keep landed estates intact from generation to generation. Some ancestor might have sweated and struggled to establish Blackacre, with the sole motive of settling it as the family seat forever.

For centuries, entailment was the principal form in which landed estates passed from one generation to another – typically, to the first-born son, leaving daughters and second-sons to fend for themselves. (Daughters hoped for husbands, second-sons had – in addition to possibly marrying money – such options as the military, the bar, and the clergy.) Clever lawyers ("conveyancers") eventually invented ways to persuade judges to dissolve ownership of this kind, allowing descendants – or their creditors – to "bar the entail" and to pledge or sell off dear Blackacre piecemeal, or all at a whack.

How people are influences *how the laws are*, and vice versa. Property relations have an influence on the behavioral ethos people exhibit. And the behavioral ethos has an influence on what property relations feature in the legal regime of a place and time. The goal of securing real political equality calls for examination of both property relations and behavioral ethos. The soloist is rightly suspicious of a purported social contract that demands changes in other people's ethics that she doubts they can live up to – to say nothing of her own readiness and capacity to alter her own attitudes to adjust to the demands of life under government.

The soloist can reflect that no one today really misses primogeniture, and entailed estates, and slavery. She knows that had she been born in another place and time, she might have dreamt of amassing land and fields and building a stately home that would stay in her family forever. The chances of realizing such a dream are now gone with the wind, as they say. She knows that some dreams are unwise, and the passing of all possibility of their coming to be real is not to be mourned, but celebrated.

Wanting to do the best one can for one's children is not a dream that can be wiped away so easily. The soloist therefore will want to look first to other adjustments in property relations, as a way to protect political equality. If changes in the property regime can serve to secure her political equality, while creating only modest strains of commitment – ones that she thinks it reasonable for each to bear – then she's all for them.

Hobbes was the first person we know of to have noticed a certain, unique category of material goods. Some things cannot usefully remain common property nor can they be divided into parcels that can usefully be owned by each, as their personal property. Of things of this nature, some are essential to living a productive life, or their products are. These are the means of production. At one time in human history, such things did not yet exist, and it is possible that in the future nothing will answer to the description. But for at least the past two centuries and for the foreseeable future, the soloist sees that she is living in "the circumstances of the means of production."

If we conceive of society as a joint endeavor for the purpose of improving everyone's material life, we implicitly join together in trying to invent new and better techniques and processes and whatever else is helpful in improving productivity. We recognize that some of these inventions will be such that they cannot usefully be everyone's personal property. We also recognize that some of these inventions will be so successful that they (or their products) will become essential (if only for a time) to participating productively in the wider economy.

Everyone can own a personal computer. Everyone can be on Facebook, and search on Google, and order on Amazon. But not everyone can own a personal Facebook, or own a personal Amazon. Dividing up Facebook the way the Homestead Act divided up the public lands in the western United States would mean no Facebook. Dividing up Amazon in a way that each person had her own private, personal piece of it would be the end of Amazon.

Everyone might have an ownership share, but that is not the same thing as having an exclusive right to the use and enjoyment of a portion of the actual enterprise. People who own shares in Coca-Cola have no right to look inside the corporate vault to examine the (mythical) formula for turning sugar water into gold. Nor do they have any right to go help themselves to a can of Diet Coke whenever they please.

The joke is told that all the physical assets of the Coca-Cola Company could be destroyed without making much of a dent in its market valuation. The brand itself is intellectual property, and it is this property – the exclusive right to market any liquid called Coca-Cola – that is the fount of the income stream that the stock market values.

The Coca-Cola brand is not something that can be owned in common: neither can it be divvied up among us all. If everyone were free to use the brand name, its value would be destroyed. The idea of dividing up the brand and distributing a usable piece of it to everyone, the way the inventory of canned beverages might be distributed, is absurd. Are Coca-Cola products widely necessary for living productively? I don't think so. Private ownership of the Coca-Cola Company is not yet an instance of private ownership of the means of production. Other things, however, unquestionably should count among the means of production.

This frames the question whether private ownership of the means of production can safely be permitted, given the soloist's grave concern to create and secure the public conditions necessary for political equality. Hobbes, who was perhaps the greatest (if also the creepiest) figure in social contract history, seemed to have thought that whatever could neither be held in common nor divided should simply go to the first to claim it or to invent it, and then descend to the first-born by the rule of primogeniture, forever and ever. Or such was his advice to the sovereign, who could either take it or leave it. We, the soloists who comprise the sovereign People, have to decide whether and how to take Hobbes's advice.

7

The Productivity Club

What assurance can any society give that each of its members will always be the political equal of every other member, regardless of their differences in other respects, such as wealth and social connections? It was clear to the soloist that this assurance has to be fixed as a background condition of any genuinely democratic process.

Like constitutional guarantees of liberty of conscience, certain matters cannot be entrusted to majority decision – certain matters are simply not for the majority to decide. Whether or not the soloist is to be treated as a political equal cannot be something that is liable to be put to a majority vote. As far as the soloist is concerned, no vote is legitimate *as to her* unless her political equality is accepted as a necessary precondition.

The two kinds of devices for protecting political equality that have been considered so far have not seemed very promising. Insulation devices do not seem suited to having constitutional status; and if referred to a legislature, they come too late. Anti-accumulation devices can take a variety of forms. Upon examination, those that involve taxation seem unsatisfactory in various ways – although they might be necessary additionally, they also seemed unfit to be cast in the role of a constitutionalized measure to assure political equality at the get-go of the legislative melee.

A constitutional exclusion of certain types of property relation was the one type of measure that seemed to stand out from the rest of the anti-accumulation measures to guarantee political equality. One such exclusion is already familiar: other kinds of unequal wealth may be tolerable, but no one may accumulate slaves. The question of whether to allow chattel slavery can never be properly brought before the legislature – it is forbidden to own slaves. (This, ironically, is almost the reverse of the situation in the U.S. Congress during much of the antebellum era: it was against the rules of order even to mention any limitation of the legal rights of slaveholders!)

Ownership of slaves was of course not a feature of a social contract to which the slaves themselves could reasonably be assumed to subscribe. Neither, for that matter, could free citizens reasonably be assumed to subscribe to a social contract that permitted unequal private wealth to accumulate in the form of slaves.

Certain types of property relation have been expressly created by their inclusion in a constitution. The U.S. Constitution, for example, authorizes the Congress to enact legislation to provide for patents and copyrights. So, determining the types of admissible property relations is not an uncommon topic for a constitution to address. That being the case, it is not unnatural to think of the social contract as, in a sense, founded on an understanding about property relations. Certain property relations can be seen as necessary or useful to social prosperity, as in the case of patents for inventions. And certain property relations can be excluded as inimical to the common weal – such as perpetuities and perpetual patents. And some property relations may be accepted by way of compromise, as in the case of chattel slavery under the U.S. Constitution of 1789.

Two questions can now be stated in a clear form: 1) Would the credibility of a promise of political equality unnecessarily be put at risk if the means of production are allowed to be privately owned? 2) Would public ownership of the means of production be a *satisfactory* (though not, alone, a sufficient) guarantee of political equality? The soloist ponders these in turn. She may be surprised that she is even asking these questions, yet now they have to be faced.

In the abstract, it is possible that productive resources, call it capital, could be distributed more-or-less equally. This fungible quantity, capital, could, at least conceivably, be spread around more-or-less continuously, so that not only had every citizen enough to enable her to contribute productively, she also had enough to keep herself on a plane of political equality with those who happened to have more capital.

Now bring the means of production into the picture. What changes is that not everyone can have their own exclusive, useful piece or parcel of this kind of asset. If the means of production are in the hands of a private owner, that private owner necessarily occupies a strategic advantage over non-owners.

The private owner could very well be, and typically is, a profit-maximizer. This means that the private owner grants access to the means of production only on terms that generate the greatest return to her. The private owner has, in fact, an incentive to do exactly that. Moreover, the private owner has an incentive to shape the cultural landscape in a way that makes her asset ever more a necessity for everyone else.

The private owner of an automobile factory, for example, may have to compete with other automakers; yet, even so, as automakers they have an incentive to have the public (with its power of eminent domain) pay to pave the landscape with roads, to have the public earmark fuel-tax revenues for roadbuilding (to the exclusion of passenger railways), and to have the public regulate land use so that the automobile becomes a necessity rather than a luxury (by requiring a certain number of parking spaces, for example, for each commercial and residential building).

Over time, the ordinary citizen has less and less effective political power vis-à-vis the automaker. The agenda for transportation policy, for example, will be determined in large part within a context already restricted by the automaker's interests. The automaker will have allies not only in competing automakers, but also in suppliers of components and raw materials, and in autoworkers and their unions. The political power of autoworkers, which might be considerable, augments that of the automaker.

Automobiles run on fuel. The owners of oil fields and refineries are also owners of the means of production. Everyone can, conceivably, own a mule or a car. But not everyone can own a network of pipelines and refineries, any more than they could own a separate stretch of highway. The highway system is publicly owned, and part of the means of production, but the petroleum industry and the auto industry are not everywhere publicly owned, even though they are, equally with the highway system, a part of today's means of production.

The automaker comes to have political influence that is far greater than that of other citizens. It is not merely that the automaker has more money. If it were simply a matter of money, redistributive taxation and insulation devices could, conceivably, serve as a corrective. What is different is that control of the means of production gives the owner a kind of political power that is distinctive not as much in its magnitude – which is great – but in the strategic advantage it gives. The social world gets remade in the image of the means of production. The horizon of human possibility is defined and its limits set by the means of production. What is politically possible is further confined within this horizon.

The advent of personal computing is a source of many similar examples. Most communities have central places where it is easier to meet up simply because that central place is where other people are likely to be hanging out anyway. Those places are usually the places where people are likely to do some shopping, simply because there are more shops. There are more shops there because it is more profitable to locate a shop where people are hanging out anyway.

Typically, town and city centers are public places. The way they are regulated and maintained is, in the more democratic societies, decided by democratic means, and the officials who administer them are accountable to the electorate.

Facebook and Amazon are the hangout and the shopping center of the digital world. They are the means of production of the online world. Just as no one could lead a fully productive life if she were physically excluded from the center of the town where she lived, so also, few today can lead fully free productive lives if excluded from the online places where people virtually meet up, or from the online marketplace where most people do their shopping.

This soloist – speaking now for myself – is not on Facebook (anymore). Other soloists, I am sure, never shop on Amazon. Doesn't this show that Facebook and Amazon are not among the means of production? I don't think so. I have no doubt that there were hardy individualists in the Old West who never rode in a rail car. Likewise, it is doubtless that there were nineteenth-century Mancunians who never saw the inside of a mine or a mill. Does this show that the railroads and the mines were not among the nineteenth-century means of production?

Not at all. That's not merely because the soloist, like Aristotle, is interested in what is true "for the most part." It is also because the soloist conceives herself as free in the sense of having a right to change her direction, to reinvent herself. The fact that women were not allowed in the mines in Victorian Britain has no tendency to show that the mines were not among the means of production. By the same token, the fact that many individuals do not drive, or fly, or shop online, does not contradict the classification of the automobile industry and the petroleum industry, the airline industry, and Amazon, as among the means of production. It is a matter of what an autonomous person would need access to, to count herself as fully free in her choice of occupation.

Suppose that, one morning, the soloist woke up and found out that a fellow citizen had bought the town center. Henceforth, it would be open for business as usual, under the private owner's management. It would be as if the town were transformed into an open-air mall. The town, in its governmental structure, might continue precisely as before.

Nonetheless, the soloist would notice that she could hardly any more consider herself the political equal of the new owner. The owner's newly gained power to use the town center itself as a means to extract the highest return changes everything. The owner's agenda will set the political agenda, going forward. The owner might even choose not to open the town square to political assemblies or pamphleteering at all.

The other citizens might oppose the owner's new power, and might outvote it. Even so, the owner's interests will disproportionately affect what there is to discuss and vote on. This would be so even if the proceeds of the sale had been distributed equally among the rest of the citizenry. It is so even if the new owner lives elsewhere, and does not even *have* a vote.

We soloists find ourselves in analogous circumstances with respect to the digital world. The information revolution that created this world was the culmination of decades of public effort to develop weapons and defenses. The myriad of civilian applications the wartime and Cold War era investments made possible were a bonanza that, it was obvious, would revolutionize the means of production.

The competitive rough-and-tumble that produced the personal computer, the smartphone, and the platforms they support, and the applications the platforms support, would almost certainly have occurred whether or not the winners were awarded ownership of creations that, in any fair analysis, were as much the people's invention as any individual entrepreneur's.

That platforms like Facebook and Amazon would arise was foreseen long before Mark Zuckerberg and Jeff Bezos became household names – even before they were born. Few citizens, of any country, can seriously consider themselves these men's political equal. The soloist does not envy their wealth or begrudge them their success. What troubles her, or should, is that the prizes they hold are of the wrong kind.

What's wrong with this kind of prize? Suppose the soloist is forced to join what I will call the *Productivity Club*. The aim of the Club is to invent ways to make labor more productive in agriculture and industry. The constitution and by-laws of the Club are not written down. Over time, the membership forms and re-forms into several teams, and the teams pursue ideas, borrowing freely from the stock of data and writing accumulating in the Club Library.

Everyone is encouraged to draw upon what is in the Library, and to try to out-do the other teams in coming up with inventions and improvements. There is a lot of trial and error, a lot of back-and-forth between teams, and the teams constantly change in number, size, and composition. Players are free to change teams. What they are not free to do is to quit playing.

One day, one of the teams, Team Rho, perfects the *Connectatron*. This device revolutionizes the way people can work and relate. Soon, everyone on all the teams is using the Connectatron. Productivity soars. Use of the Connectatron platform and access across the Connectatron network quickly become essential to being a productive worker.

Who owns the Connectatron? Team Rho, who perfected it? Team Alpha, who first thought of it (they claim)? Team Beta, who (you guessed it…) first tested the Connectatron? Or Team Psi, who has made the cleverest use of it?

Or is there something mistaken about the premise of the

question, which is that some one of the teams owns the Connectatron, to the exclusion of all others? After all, the whole point of the Productivity Club was to improve productivity. If each team – no, better – if each *person* could own a personal Connectatron, then everyone could look forward to owning one, the same way everyone could someday own a smartphone. But if the Connectatron belongs among the means of production, there is no possibility of its being severally owned.

Let's stipulate that the Connectatron is a network, forming a platform that cannot be severally owned. It is not like an iPhone or an Android device, but like Facebook, or Amazon. Facebook would not be Facebook, and Amazon would not be Amazon, if they were not the place to connect – so also with the Connectatron. Even if the Connectatron could be broken into, say, half a dozen chunks, that would not be nearly enough to go around, and cutting it into enough bits to go around would kill it altogether.

Customarily, each team in the Club gets to own and sell what it manufactures. Team Rho wants to charge everyone for access to the Connectatron, and there are objections that things like the Connectatron should be jointly owned by everybody. The constitution and by-laws of the Productivity Club, we've assumed, are unwritten. The members of the Club have to decide *what's fair*.

Recall that exiting the Productivity Club in protest is not an option. There is no other club. Recall too that everyone was forced to join the Productivity Club. They entered it by being born, and they exit it only when they die. Perhaps there ought to have been a rule applicable to the means of production stated at the outset. It is too late for that. The question now is, is there some rule that it would have been unreasonable to reject had it been proposed when the Productivity Club started up?

Here's an interesting actual case that might shed some light on the issue. In a town in south Alabama there is a Waffle House restaurant. A customer, a Mr. Edward

Seward, liked to tip the members of the wait staff who happened to wait on him by giving them lottery tickets. Seward was in the habit of buying these tickets in the neighboring state of Florida, because Alabama (back then) had no lottery and outlawed gambling. The wait staff – there were five of them – were happy to be tipped this way, one ticket apiece, even though the chances of winning the lottery were extremely slim.

One day, one of the tickets Seward bought, and tipped with, turned out to be a winner, worth roughly $5,000,000. The holder of the winning ticket happened to be Tonda Dickerson. Dickerson wasted no time submitting the ticket and putting the proceeds into a Subchapter S corporation formed for the purpose, apparently, of making it harder for her fellow wait-persons at the Waffle House to succeed in getting hold of any of it.

The other four filed a lawsuit, praying for one-fifth of the lottery proceeds for each. The basis of their claim, in essence, was that there was an informal understanding that they would share equally if any of the tickets Seward was using to tip paid off. Pooling tips is often the practice at restaurants, and the plaintiffs convinced a trial jury that there was an oral agreement among the five that winnings from the lottery tickets would be pooled that way, if any ever materialized.

The jury returned a plaintiffs' verdict. On appeal, the judgment was reversed, on the ground that the agreement was a gambling contract and thus void under Alabama law. There are further, fascinating details that, sadly, cannot be expounded here. I mention the case to throw relief on an issue that concerns us all, even though we have never waited tables at the Waffle House in Grand Bay, Alabama.

Leave aside the question whether the five wait staff had reached an actual, explicit agreement about what to do in case one of the tickets paid off. What would have been reasonable to propose? Since it could not be known in advance which of the five would be given a winning ticket (in the highly improbable event that any of them were), none of the five could propose a rule favoring themselves vis-à-vis the others.

Tonda Dickerson, in this hypothetical circumstance, might have proposed a winner-take-all rule. If the others could not propose a better rule than winner-take-all, then they could hardly complain that it was unfair or unjust for Dickerson to take all when Seward dealt her the winning ticket (his habit was to place each ticket in a separate sealed envelope).

The obvious alternative to winner-take-all is a rule of share-and-share-alike. Is pooling so clearly superior to winner-take-all that it would be unreasonable to reject it? That is not clear to me.

The case of the Productivity Club is similar in some ways to the Waffle House Lottery case, and different in others. In both cases, the people involved are working toward a common goal. In the Waffle House case, pleasing Mr. Seward was important to all five of the wait staff. If Seward stopped coming or stopped tipping, there would be no lottery tickets.

In both cases, all concerned have an incentive to be productive, apart from the prize in question. In the Waffle House case, the wait staff are paid (I'd guess) the minimum wage plus cash tips. It seems unlikely that the difference between a slim chance of winning $5 million, and an almost equally slim chance of winning $1 million, could convey a significantly greater incentive to be nice to Mr. Seward.

The members of the Productivity Club are paid a market wage. There are those who would love nothing more than to revolutionize the means of production – merely coming up with new products does not satisfy them. But, for *some* of these special soloists, suppose there would be no point to revolutionizing the means of production *unless* they would then own them. A higher salary, a bonus, prestige, fame, gratitude, honors – none of that would do.

Is it plausible to think that offering ownership of the

means of production as the prize for revolutionizing the means of production is *uniquely* necessary to incentivize the revolutionaries, the creative geniuses? That gobs of money, medals, book contracts, and so forth, just won't call forth the socially necessary effort? That the very best soloists will simply sit on the sidelines and sulk?

This seems dubious. Does anyone think that the end of entailed estates diminished the acquisitive zeal of English society? That the world lost a Marconi or a Tesla who would have revolutionized the world but for the Rule against Perpetuities?

In fact, it is astonishing how small a part material incentives *of any sort* have played in the lives of people like Alexander Graham Bell (the telephone) or Jack Kilby (the integrated circuit). So, there seems to be no good reason to think that an incentive *in the peculiarly alluring form* of the possibility of private ownership of the means of production is needed to induce innovation.

Enough, for the moment, about upside incentives. Look now at downside risks.

In the Waffle House case, it is hard to gauge whether there is a greater downside risk under the winner-take-all rule or the share-and-share-alike rule. The worst outcome under share-and-share alike might be that nobody gets a winning ticket. Or it might be that someone gets a winning ticket and, as a result, everyone's life is ruined, as so commonly happens to lottery winners. (Don't dismiss this as owing only to the culture shock of going from nothing to the big-time. Jack Whittaker was already worth $17 million when he won – to his ruin – a Powerball lump sum amounting to $113.4 million after taxes.) Set this risk aside (or is the thrill of playing the lottery like the thrill of hang-gliding, in which the chance of breaking one's neck is part of the fun?).

Let's say the worst outcome under winner-takes-all might be having someone else on the wait staff win, and having to envy all the wonderful things the lucky one can now afford. The badness of this could, possibly, be mitigated by the *schadenfreude* of watching the lucky winner's life blow up. (Mitigated, or entirely canceled out!)

Although it is hard to say which of winner-take-all and share-and-share alike has the worse downside in the Waffle House case, either rule has a less bad downside than a rule of "let's take a vote after one of us wins." Under that rule, the holder of the winning ticket is likely to insist on winner-take-all, and the others to vote for share-and-share-alike. Does majority rule, or is consensus needed? John Rawls warned about what happens when "basic agreements are made too late" (1999b: 225).

The three alternative rules that can be proposed in the Productivity Club case are these: 1) The means of production must be owned privately, in the same way other kinds of thing are privately owned. 2) The means of production *may* be privately owned, on such terms as a majority of the Club membership decides from time to time. 3) The means of production must be the joint property of all members of the Club, managed according to the general direction of the Club majority.

The differences in the incentive effects of the three options do not initially appear to be any more significant in the Club case than in the Waffle House case. So we ask, which of the three options in the Club case carries the worst downside risk?

If the downside risk of a given option is non-trivial and very bad, and its upside risk is not much better than what is already likely, then that option carries what we can call an *intolerable risk*. The soloist, rational being that she is, will avoid options carrying an intolerable risk if she has another option whose downside is not so very bad. Being also reasonable, she will not propose to others that they enter into an arrangement that unnecessarily imposes an intolerable risk upon any of them.

In the Waffle House case, the let's-not-decide-until-the-issue-is-pressing option risked the worst outcome (in the actual case, years of acrimony, litigation, and eventual violence). The analogous option in the Club case is the second option, to let the membership decide from time to time what to do.

Historically, the issue has not always been important enough to be worth worrying about. Until the Industrial Revolution, nothing much fell into the means-of-production category. In the future, the Club might someday perfect a cheap tabletop 3D personal printer that can produce anything you can think of out of thin air, on voice command. *The* means of production (with that portentous definite article) will then have vanished.

Now, though, we are in circumstances in which new means of production have appeared and transformed the relations of production during our own lifetimes. Like the wait staff at Waffle House, we wish we had settled what to do in this case before a settlement became so urgent. Our Club would be wise to settle it before each member has already found out what best serves his personal interest.

Can the Club's democratic character survive if the rule is: the team that revolutionizes the means of production gets to own it? In a formal sense, the rule of one member/ one vote can survive. Changing the rule requires a super-majority, and the winning team will have the resources and leverage to discourage any initiative to change.

When the means of production are privately owned, the owners have an incentive to extract rents from everyone else. Those rents are additional to what the owners can command in the market for their labor. The rents add to economic inequality. Moreover, the private owners of the means of production get to make a range of decisions about the character of the community, without needing the community's approval. That's part-and-parcel of ownership.

Suppose, for example, that the Connectatron produces a certain amount of pollution, which varies directly with the number of hours it operates. Were the question put to a membership vote, the Club would consider how best to balance the benefit of extra hours of availability against the harm done by the pollutants. Were the question instead solely for the private owner to decide, the chief consideration would be how to maximize the extraction of rents from the Connectatron.

Where to dispose of Connectatron pollutants that cannot simply be spewed into the air or dumped into the river? These pollutants go into landfill, but which land? The Rho Team will be inclined to dump them where land is cheapest. This happens to be in the neighborhood of where the least wealthy Club members reside. Whether this location would be unfair is an issue that would be pressed vigorously if the Club as a whole were to decide. If the decision is left to the Rho Team alone to make, it might be vented too, but probably not as vigorously. The Rho Team mostly lives in Rho Estates, far away from the dump site.

Once the dump is sited, the costs of relocating it will be great – so great that discussions within the Club about where to put future waste will be shaped by the fact that the Rho Team has already made a choice. The baseline for future choices for the entire Club has now been set by a minority of its members. The cherished political equality of the membership begins to sound hollow.

Imagine that the Connectatron can carry advertising. The ad revenue could greatly benefit the team that owns the Connectatron, even though the ads would mostly mean added distraction and annoyance for users. Using the Connectatron is a necessity, so exposure to advertising becomes a necessity too, but only because the team owning the Connectatron dictates that it be so. Hey – it's *their* Connectatron.

Information about individual users of the Connectatron is useful to advertisers. The Connectatron owner can maximize ad revenue by enabling advertisers to tailor and target their ads. As the owner, the team that controls the Connectatron could simply require users to consent in advance to the collection and use of personal information. That seems like a heavy-handed thing to do; but, hey – it's *their* Connectatron.

The non-owners who are unhappy with how the owners are running the Connectatron can always make proposals to regulate it. Let's assume the owners are few and the non-owners are many. Won't majority rule assure the same balance will be reached as would be reached if all were joint owners? Likely, not.

In the nature of the thing, under private ownership the typical non-owner has less to gain from a successful regulatory proposal than the owners stand to lose from it. Conversely, under private ownership, the owners have more to gain, individually, from a successful deregulatory proposal than non-owners, individually, have to lose from it. Pursuit of the collective good – which is merely the aggregate of individual goods – is likely to be overwhelmed by the strategic advantage enjoyed by the owners of the means of production.

Now suppose, to the contrary of the above, that the means of production are always to be held and managed as the joint property of everyone in the Club. The political equality of the membership is manifest in the setup itself. There is less incentive to try to extract rents from the Connectatron. All must pay them equally, or in the measure decided democratically, among political equals. There is less temptation to externalize the harms and costs incident to operating the Connectatron. Avoidance of the costs will be to no one's particular benefit. The costs will be shared equally, or in the measure decided democratically among political equals.

The Connectatron reshapes the social world each member of the Club inhabits. The shape it assumes is no longer an accidental result of the rent-seeking behavior of the members of the Rho Team. It is the result of the democratic decisions of the Club as a whole. These decisions might be wise or foolish, impulsive or considered, and in fact many of them might be similar to those the Rho Team would make. What is different about them, essentially, is that now the decisions and their consequences can truly be said to belong to each of the members of the Club, and not merely to those who supported them.

The moral of this extended tale is this. If a soloist had a chance to choose a constitution for the Productivity Club, she would choose the one that best protected her basic rights and her political equality rather than the one that allowed for awarding the greatest prize. Her basic rights do not include a right to win *bigtime*. That is, they do not include a right to win a prize so stupendous that it undermines the stability of the Club itself. They do not include a right to win a prize so huge that it eclipses the confidence of other members in their political equality.

When it comes to the question of the means of production, she realizes that everyone can become better off as these means are improved, even revolutionized. But she has no reason to want to own them, per se. The possibility of gaining personal ownership of the means of production, per se, is as unnecessary to stimulate innovation in economic life as is the allurement of gaining personal ownership of the government, or of the whole world. The soloist is not a megalomaniac.

Recognizing the unique importance of the means of production, the soloist is attentive to the risks inherent in their private ownership. Private ownership not only permits the accumulation of rents, and hence, dramatically larger degrees of material inequality, it also gives the private owner a strategic advantage over non-owners in matters of government. The public power becomes, to a repugnant degree, a private utility.

The argument I am pressing comes to this: a soloist would no more agree to a social contract that would allow private ownership of the means of production than she, as a member of the Productivity Club, would agree to a rule that would allow the Connectatron to become the private property of Team Rho. To agree to it would be to take an intolerable risk, namely, the risk that she could lose her equal voice in determining what her social world will become, and with that, in determining what kind of

person she can and her children can become, and what
dreams it will make sense for her to think they are free to
pursue.

She can be forced to take this risk, but she will have to
be. As long as there is an alternative to taking an unreasonable risk, she can reasonably reject it. Socialism is that
alternative.

Is socialism a real alternative in the world as we find
it? The means of production are, most of them, most
everywhere, in private hands. Those who own the means
of production have disproportionate political power. The
window of discourse does not, yet, include taking the means
of production into public ownership. There are exceptions
to this. There is an increasing push in the U.K. to roll back
the piecemeal privatization of the National Health Service,
which even the Conservative Party officially reveres, and
to re-nationalize the railways.

It is more common, however, to hear about initiatives
to "Tax Amazon," rather than to nationalize it; or to
shame Facebook into curbing its exploitative behavior,
rather than to take control of it. Compare the fate of the
British East India Company, a private corporation, whose
abuses of the native population of India led to Parliament's
taking it over in the nineteenth century. We today forget
that corporations are merely artificial persons, and that
the corporate form, with its limitation of investor liability,
was created in order to advance public purposes.

Anyway, how could the means of production be taken
into public ownership except by the draconian method of
outright confiscation? An historical example, in Sweden,
shows how. It also shows how difficult it is for popular
majorities to overcome the resistance of entrenched private
owners of the means of production.

In the latter half of the twentieth century, two Swedish
economists, Rudolf Meidner and Gösta Rehn, proposed a
20 percent tax on corporate profits, payable not in cash
but in new stock, and payable not to the state treasury, but
to a wage-earner fund administered by a consortium of

labor unions. This Meidner Plan, as it came to be known, would have led to the gradual acquisition of a controlling interest in all major corporations by the trade unions.

Olof Palme won the Swedish election in 1982 on a platform that endorsed the Meidner Plan. As prime minister, Palme initiated the implementation of a diluted variant of the Plan, which took the form of an excess-profits tax, payable to regional public funds for the purpose of buying shares of Swedish corporations. The program was brought to an abrupt end following Palme's party's loss in the 1991 election. The funds had, by that time, acquired about 7 percent of Swedish corporate stock. (Palme himself had been assassinated in 1986.)

Palme's election in 1982 elicited an almost hysterical reaction in the finance-friendly press internationally. Swedish capitalists directed their opposition through the Federation of Swedish Industry, an already existing organ-ization that had been created to defend their interests. Resistance to the "Socialist takeover" was lavishly funded and had the volunteered support of Sweden's internationally known soft-pop band, ABBA ("Money, Money, Money," "Winner Takes It All"). The band said it would be forced to take its $200-million-a-year financial empire elsewhere, "London, Los Angeles, or New York." ("Mamma Mia!")

Nevertheless, wage-earner funds have flourished across the globe in succeeding decades. In 2019, *The Economist* reported a poll showing that "about 55% of American voters support putting up to half of a company's shares in a trust for workers. Even 50% of Republicans support such a scheme, with only 30% opposed." *Executive* compensation in the form of stock in the company is commonplace – so why not also for laborers?

In this century, repeated financial crises have left states owning whole industries. The 2008 "Great Recession," for example, dropped the financial sector, the automotive industry, and the re-insurance industry of the United States into the public lap. President Obama, in deference to American traditions sanctifying private ownership, hastened to re-privatize these means of production by lavishing (further) public subsidies upon them. Popular resentment of these massive bailouts, and the failure to hold private managements accountable, has contributed to an erosion of public trust in governments over the ensuing decade.

The crises that are current at this writing can be an occasion for the People to reconsider whether they are now ready to keep hold of what history keeps trying to return to them.

8

Managing Public Assets

The soloist insists upon her autonomy and her independence. Nothing galls her quite as much as the sense that she is being dominated, bossed, pushed around. Tyranny was the by-product of civilization, as Rousseau told the story. In a true state of nature,

> A man might seize the fruits another has picked, the game he has killed, the lair he used for shelter; but how will he ever succeed in getting himself obeyed by him, and what would be the chains of dependence among men who possess nothing? If I am chased from one tree, I just go to another one. If I am tormented in one place, who will keep me from going somewhere else? Is there a man so superior to me in strength, and, in addition, is so depraved, so lazy, and so ferocious as to force me to provide for his subsistence while he remains idle? (Rousseau 1755: II, I, 48)

What caused this era to end, if – as Rousseau claimed – it was humanity's happiest and longest lasting? In two words, agriculture and *cooperation*:

> as long as they applied themselves only to tasks a single individual could perform and to arts that did not require the collaboration of several hands, they lived free, healthy,

good, and happy as far as they could by their nature be, and continued to enjoy the gentleness of independent dealings with one another; but the moment one man needed the help of another; as soon as it was found useful for one to have provisions for two, equality disappeared, property appeared, work became necessary, and vast forests changed into smiling Fields that had to be watered with the sweat of men, and where slavery and misery were soon seen to sprout and grow together with the harvests. (II, II, 19)

Although hunting already called on occasions for coordinated activity, cultivating the soil from season to season imposes drastically greater demands on the formerly free-spirited gatherer. Continuous cooperation among equals is hard to arrange. Rousseau thought it was possible, though his solution will seem suspicious to the soloist. It has something to do with forming a "general will," over and above the sum of individual wills. When the individual wills something other than the general will, well, she must be "forced to be free," for her true will is expressed, now, not by the voice in her own head, but by the general will.

The soloist shrugs off this story. Even so, she can feel the pull of the idea that if her basic rights are respected, and she is truly a political equal, then a majority may legitimately make decisions about the detailed terms of cooperation. As a political equal, she may be outvoted without having thereby been dominated.

Rousseau was conscious that his reverie could not be realized in the conditions of the feudal vassal, or the commoner faced with the choice between indentured servitude or starvation. The European discovery of America offered what seemed to be a blank slate upon which a social contract might be drafted anew. The U.S. Constitution of 1789 simultaneously aroused and dashed the hope of a new birth of liberty.

On the eve of the coming Civil War, Lincoln extolled the Wisconsin farmers and took their side in their struggle against the money-kings, whose tyranny was as palpable as that of the crown-king against whom the Founding generation had made revolt. The steam plow was the key to independence and productivity. When the war broke out, the money-kings persuaded Lincoln to give them the railroad, the means of production by which a united continent would be submitted to its most thorough cultivation.

The farmer's dependence on the banks was compounded by their new dependence on the railroad-kings. Even so, the dream of the sturdy, independent frontier farmer still has a grip on the imagination of politicians and those who hearken to their rhetoric. Beneath the rhetoric was the reality that the farmer on the plains was as subservient to capital as any proletarian toiling in a Manchester mill.

Socialism promises to secure everyone's political equality by making everyone an equal, joint owner of the means of production. The skeptical soloist wants to know how, exactly, she can be a political equal if these means of production are managed as public assets. Under socialism (why "under"?) will she not have simply traded one set of bosses for another?

Socialism, to her, connotes a centralized governmental bureaucracy. Public assets can hardly be managed by an assembly of the whole, or by referendum. Managers will have to be chosen. True, they should be elected (for fixed terms), and might be subject to recall. If that is the case then management is more responsive to the public than is so with privately owned assets. Private corporations can be set up in various ways, but the typical case involves a class of voting shareholders that from time to time, by majority voting, elect a board of directors, who, by majority vote, hire and remove the firm's principal officers. The employees, and the public, are outsiders.

Public ownership of the means of production is appealing, in large part, for two reasons. First, the public is not necessarily interested in maximizing the rents derived from the assets it holds. Second, private owners of those same assets would normally insist that management maximize the rents that can be extracted from the firm's assets. That's what maximizes "shareholder value," and private investors pick among, buy, hold and sell shares in order to maximize the expected value of the dividends to be paid out of revenues to shareholders.

Managers of private corporations want to please the boards of directors that hire them. Managers therefore want to maximize shareholder value, over whatever interval of time the market for shares seems to care about. That interval can be very short. If there is a market for shares then shareholders are free to sell up and take their money wherever they think they can get a higher return. Thus, shareholders have no reason to care what the shares will be worth in twenty years, say. Or even twenty days. All they have reason to care about is knowing when it is time to get out.

Managers of public assets also want to please those who have hired them and can fire them. Accountability means liability to losing one's job. In a socialist economy, every citizen is a shareholder in the means of production. But their shares are not tradable. Therefore, citizens have no reason to be concerned about the price of their shares relative to other investments they might make. Managers of public assets are judged not on the basis of market valuation. They are judged on the basis of how well the assets are fulfilling the purpose the public has chosen for them to serve, as judged by the People (with a capital "P").

One common misconception about socialism is that it dispenses altogether with markets. Markets can be a wonderful source of information, the soloist recalls from ECON 101. Without markets and revenues, a firm that engages in selling goods or services lacks the best evidence of all about how well it is doing its job. This means that the managers of the firm are to that extent unaccountable, because the owners – the People – cannot with one glance at the books see whether the firm is wasting resources. A socialist economy will surely include a consumer sector, and in this sector, at least, the absence of competition in the market means that there is no easy way to tell whether the firm is being managed efficiently – much like the case with a monopoly in a capitalist economy.

This eventuality is not merely unfortunate, as inefficiencies often are: it is unfortunate in a special way. The soloist has been invited to buy into socialism as the best way to secure her political equality. Yet now it appears that there is an inherent asymmetry of information as between managers and ordinary citizens. Without competitive markets it is almost impossible for ordinary citizens to tell how good a job management is doing; while managers, as insiders, have plenty more information.

As far as the direction of the public asset goes, the influence of the management class is at least as great as that of the despised and now-banished capitalist class. It would be pedantic, as well as self-contradictory, to deny that this inequality is effectively also an inequality of political influence. The managers, with their superior access to information, decide the political agenda. In doing so, they exercise outsized influence over the shape of the common world. Socialism's advantage over its alternatives is *nada*, as judged in terms of the achievement of political equality.

The response to this very real worry is to remind the soloist that social ownership of the means of production need not involve consolidating or centralizing the economy. The economy's "commanding heights" will be publicly owned and democratically controlled. That, however, leaves much of, if not most of, the economy in private hands. Everything from kitchenware and clothing to coffee shops and gyms flourishes in the hands of and under the direction of private firms, competing for clients and customers. Recall that the means of production consist only of those things that meet, or whose products meet, two criteria: they cannot be parceled out to all and they are widely necessary to making a living.

The means of production comprise such things as the

power grid, the telecommunications network, the online retail hub, the transportation system, and the financial system. Even here, there is no necessity that these sectors be consolidated. The economist John Roemer has outlined how competition can work in a publicly owned banking system. Instead of having one big central bank, there can be multiple banks, under independent management, all subject to public oversight. Within this competitive framework, banks as lenders have an incentive to discipline their borrowers. This discipline is subservient, however, to public purposes, rather than to maximizing private shareholder-value.

The banking sector as a whole, in a socialist economy, deliberately subsidizes activities that the public as a whole selects, democratically, as a priority. (Capitalist economies subsidize, too. Bailouts aside, the Anglo-American law of property, trusts, and corporations has itself been called "the mother of all subsidies" [Pistor 2019: 222]). Healthcare can be provided free of charge in a socialist economy because healthcare is not expected to pay for itself. Health is unambiguously a good. Rare cases of clinical hypochondria and Munchausen Syndrome are not good evidence of any "moral hazard" attendant to free provision of basic healthcare.

Other provisions of the means of production, by comparison, may be such that the public would be better served by charges intended to curtail consumption. Electricity, for example, or internet access. Public ownership of the means of production need not entail excluding competition; it need not entail provision upon demand, free of charge; it need not entail comprehensive planning.

Socialism does *allow* for comprehensive planning, of course. Which is a good thing. When a certain means of production creates externalities – costs not automatically borne by the producer – then the socially optimal result can be the retirement or replacement of that means. Private owners interested only in profits have an incentive to conceal what they know about these costs, and to resist public efforts to shift or discourage consumer demand for what they have to sell. Private owners, generally, have an incentive to encourage consumers, generally, to think of themselves *as* consumers – not as citizens – when spending their incomes. When the public owns an enterprise, citizens have an incentive to consider both the public cost as well as the individual benefit its activities involve.

These incentives aren't always enough. The problem of fossil fuels and global heating is an illustration. Compare two petroleum producing nations, Venezuela and Norway. In both, the petroleum industry is a public asset. In both, the revenue from the extraction of petroleum is a main source of state revenue. In both, it is known that the well-being of future generations of citizens is jeopardized by continuing the use of fossil fuels. Venezuela has done nothing to reduce its dependence on fossil fuels or its dependence on the exploitation and export of its reserves still in the ground. By contrast, Norway has taken significant steps to wean itself off fossil fuels, although none (as yet) toward leaving its petroleum reserves in the ground and under the seabed.

The contrast shows that public ownership, per se, is no guarantee that the state will wisely manage the means of production. Socialism is not a panacea. Yet social ownership enables Norway to move away from fossil fuel use; and curtailing exploration and extraction is a live political issue. Compare, now, Norway and Alaska, one of the United States. Alaska, similarly to Norway, has a social-wealth fund holding assets derived from petroleum production. The privately owned petroleum industry, despite its "greenwashing" public-relations fluff to the contrary, is committed to the continued exploitation of public lands in Alaska and the extraction of petroleum in the pursuit of profits. Private ownership of the means of production in the United States makes Norwegian-style responsibility politically precarious in Alaska.

It is true that Norway's petroleum reserves are managed

by experts. It is also surely true that as Norway moves toward a carbon-neutral economy, the influence of those experts should diminish. These suppositions, however, fail to show that – presently and in the interim – political equality among Norwegians is a facade, or that Norway's economic policy is dictated by a managerial elite. In fact, they show the reverse.

What about life within the firm? The socialism discussed so far has not touched on the question of democracy within economic units, whether publicly or privately owned. The soloist has been sold on the idea that justice demands political equality, and she has been sensitized to the insidious frauds so often committed under the guise of merely formal political equality. She is expected to make a living in a competitive economy, and to accept economic inequalities as just fine as they are. She is expected to trim her pursuit of her dreams to her budget, and to accept responsibility for the shortfalls.

She is expected to accept the legitimacy of this system in exchange for the assurance that it treats her as a political equal. And yet, the political equality the soloist was assured begins to look pretty thin if she cannot take it with her into the workplace. Where she works, typically, she is subject to *private government*, as philosopher Elizabeth Anderson calls it. The soloist has to spend up to a third of her day, and sometimes more, subject to managerial dictatorship. Where is her political equality now?

The soloist had thought that socialism meant liberation from being bossed by others, if it meant anything. The "liberal, democratic" socialism offered up in these pages looks to be a bait-and-switch deal, unless the democratic bit applies in her workplace as well as outside.

It does apply, although not across the board, to all firms, or in a uniform way. The means of production are of such great importance to everyone that all must have a say in setting their general course. The financial sector is among the means of production, but that sector cannot be left to be governed solely by those employed in it, even if – internally – governance is perfectly democratic. A process of governing may be democratic as to those included in it and yet dictatorial as to those outside.

As to certain matters, each person in a liberal society gets to be the dictator. What you think, how you decorate your body, and so on – that's up to you. There can be reasonable differences about what is and isn't included within this private sphere. Even so, there is a core of agreement that, for example, each person gets to dictate their hair color. So also in a liberal socialist society, where the means of production are a thing that nobody and no sub-group can ever be the dictator of. Private ownership of the means of production is viewed by socialists as off the table, the same way chattel slavery is off the table.

Besides the means of production, a liberal socialist society contains a vast variety of associations, business firms, unions, sports clubs, affinity groups, religious cults, and so on. Their internal government may be but need not be democratic. Even so, a socialist society will encourage cooperatives and similar types of employee-owned enterprises. The basic right to freedom of association includes the power to enter into contracts of employment that involve surrendering to the dictatorship of supervisors (who, in turn, can be dictated to by managers).

The basic liberties of occupational choice and self-determination protect the possibility of voluntarily entering a wage relation with a private firm. The owner of the firm is free to use his resources to build a business; and non-owners are free to exchange their labor-power for money. As long as the wider economy contains a wide range of alternative employment opportunities, the employment relation is not unjust per se.

Similarly, if there is a sufficient variety of other employment opportunities in the economy, there is no principled reason to object to the wage relation existing within firms that manage the means of production. What socialists insist upon is that the public dictate the goals and broad direction of those firms, and that the public itself receive the dividends (if any) that the firm generates.

In short, Walter the nurse is free to quit his nursing job and start a bakery. He is free to hire Ned and Shontay, and they are free to work for him. Walter is free to insist on "being the boss," and to insist that he keep the entire profits of the enterprise. Ned and Shontay are free to push back, to associate, to strike, and to quit. Socialist labor law will regulate how Walter can deal with his employees; but no sane socialist will insist on workplace democracy and employee ownership so rigidly as to discourage Walter the nurse from becoming Walter the baker. The idea of socialism is to free Walter, Ned, Shontay, and Helga to become what they want to be.

A democratically directed financial sector may choose to offer incentives, in the form of favorable credit terms, to persuade Walter to set up his bakery as an employee cooperative. Employee cooperatives are often successes even in non-socialist economies, yet it has to be acknowledged that the co-op form has its disadvantages. For example, co-ops may be slower to hire than Walter the sole proprietor would be, since the value of every existing employee's share is diluted by each new hire a co-op makes.

It would be unwise for the finance sector to make incentives to co-ops so great as to effectively compel Walter's choice. It would be unjust as well as unwise to make the co-op form mandatory throughout the economy. Socialists like to have a choice of boutiques on their Main Streets and High Streets as much as anyone. And they cherish their liberty to open them.

Political equality presents itself now as even more central to the social contract. Government is legitimate only if it is consented to at the fundamental level and if, as to less fundamental matters, the soloist cannot reasonably reject government by a majority with which she disagrees. The workplace tests the soloist even further, insofar as even majority rule is likely to be absent within many if not most of the firms apt to hire her.

The social contract asks her not only to accept economic inequality but also to accept power differentials in the workplace, knowing she may find herself on the short end of both. This is a big ask, and would be too much to ask of her outside a system of institutions in which her political equality was assured in matters properly subject to democratic control.

Socialism, as it is now best understood, took definite form as a response to the Industrial Revolution. That event marked the world-historical arrival of the means of production and the coordinate disappearance of any prospect of maintaining the sturdy independence that Lincoln thought within reach of everybody, on small, thoroughly cultivated agrarian homesteads.

The essential means of living a productive life today cannot usefully remain as an unrestricted commons, nor can they be divided into usable, individually owned parcels. Hobbes was the first to recognize this distinctive type of ownable thing. Although he was a pioneer in asserting people's natural equality, Hobbes, notoriously, cared not a whit for their political equality. So, it is no surprise that his insouciant advice to the sovereign favored unequal private ownership of the whole of such things.

As the social contract gets spelled out, a clause addressing the means of production will absolutely have to be included. The soloist appreciates that the means of production, and revolutions within that category, will radically shape and reshape her social world. She knows she cannot hope to be the political equal of private owners of the means of production. Public ownership of the means of production, by itself, is not a sufficient guarantee of political equality, but it is a necessary one.

To allow private ownership is not only to award an excessive prize that no one can claim to deserve to have, it is also to risk the private owner's capturing two of the three vital parts of the democratic political process. On the front end, private owners threaten to set the political agenda; on the back end, they can threaten a capital strike – or in a global economy, capital flight – that is, to withdraw their vital capital assets to thwart the implementation of popular laws. In a perverse feedback loop, the back-end threat, or even the possibility of it, narrows the window of discourse on the front end. This leaves only the middle, one-person/one-vote electoral part standing securely – as mere window dressing.

A good empirical case has been made that, in developed countries, increasing economic and social inequality is correlated with a number of undesirable social consequences, in terms of life expectancy, health, happiness, violence, and trust (see Wilkinson and Pickett 2010). A soloist values her personal liberty so far as not to consent to its subjection to a calculus of social interest that would restrict her basic rights, even if she would likely be happier. The case for socialism should rest on the sounder footing that it is an essential element of any durable guarantee of her political equality. The distinctive, threshold measure that socialism takes to guarantee political equality is public ownership of the means of production. It is not sufficient, by itself, but it is objectively ascertainable whether it has been taken. Other prescriptions, which attempt freehandedly to "compress" or right-size the distance between the classes, lack this objectivity. They are less effective as constitutional safeguards.

In sum, the soloist's choice comes to this: which of two frameworks for managing the means of production poses the greater risk to her political equality? In the first framework, she is necessarily a voting shareholder. She has the power to propose initiatives, stand as a candidate for office, as well as to vote. In the second framework, she probably has no vote and no equity ownership. If she has enough money, and shares are publicly traded, she might be able to amass a controlling bloc of voting shares – and if not, even her share ownership leaves her without a real say. ("Vote management or sell" is the standard advice given to unhappy minority stockholders.)

The far greater risk evidently lies with the second

framework, in which the means of production are privately owned. Were this a mere matter of diversifying a portfolio, the soloist might be contented to hedge her bet by letting the ownership question be decided by majority vote. Unfortunately, that strategy leads to the worst option, in this context. It means leaving the decision to ordinary politics when it becomes pressing. That is like what the Waffle House wait staff did, and it was a disaster.

Conclusion: Summarizing the Soloist Case for Socialism

If political society is conceived as a fair system of cooperation for mutual benefit, what could justify private ownership of the means of production? Nothing, really.

Setting things up so that successful people have a chance to own the means of production is unnecessary to stimulate innovation. The world is a happier place without perpetuities and the entail, so also it should be without capitalism. Let the successful bequeath the bulk of their estates, so long as the means of production are secure in the people's collective hands.

Once a subset of society gets title to the means of production, those excluded from that subset cannot be expected to think of themselves as the political equals of those on the inside. Private owners of the means of production are a class apart. A political society conceived as a fair productive venture intended to benefit all would not be set up that way.

How *do* we conceive of political society? Philosopher and life-long socialist Jerry Cohen proposed we think of it as a camping trip. Free-market economist Friedrich von Hayek would suggest we think of a poker weekend. If we are together on a camping trip, we should expect to share what we bring and share more-or-less equally in the fun and the work it involves. If we are having a poker weekend, we expect to do some sharing, but winning is the name of the game. Which of these analogies grabs us would largely determine what principles of justice we think should govern our political institutions. If political society is like a camping trip, some kind of socialism seems inescapable. But if political society is like a poker weekend, we have no ground to complain if, come Monday morning, the winner has taken it all.

A better theory of justice is premised on a different conception of political society. Recognizing that we have no real option but to take part, we can nonetheless think of society as a cooperative system for mutual benefit. As free equals, we each have our own aims, which can conflict; but we know we can better achieve our aims by submission to rules for managing conflicts and for dividing the benefits that cooperation brings. Are there any rules we would be willing to stick to if everyone else will? If there are such rules, they would define a conception of justice for our society; and, if the rules are enforceable by serious pressures, then they define a conception of political justice.

The rules that emerge will not be the same as those for a camping trip. A camping trip is not intended to produce what will sustain society for generations. We take what we need with us – it is already in existence. If one of us has forgotten to bring something, we share, which means others sacrifice. A poker weekend lets chance and skill decide how what we bring to the table gets divided. If one player takes all, that's not unfair. But if we throw in together to produce what we need in order to live full lives, we will choose different rules. Manna does not descend from heaven; if it did, equal division might be fair. Once we think of society as a productive system, we will not insist on equal division if assured that an unequal division leaves all of us better off in absolute terms.

The natural talents we possess individually have what social value they have, if any, depending upon how they are valued by others. The contribution our individual efforts make to social wealth cannot intelligibly be factored into several portions. Markets decide what, if anything, our efforts are socially worth. The inequalities that result from using markets are ones we accept, but only supposing all benefit by the system. It would be irrational to accept a principle of winner-takes-all when we view society as proposed here. Even if one were confident that one would be that winner, or hungered for that main chance, one would be unreasonable in proposing winner-takes-all to others, for they could reasonably reject it.

We will insist upon certain rights – such as freedom of conscience, freedom of occupational choice, and freedom of association – as having a prior position with respect to whatever principle we adopt for dividing the social surplus. Even if everyone were to benefit materially, it would be unjust to force Helga the pulmonologist to work 80 hours a week – or even to force her to stay at medicine as a career. We will insist on a right to personal property, the tools of our trade, and perhaps on owning a home. We will insist on equality of economic opportunity.

We reach the crucial question of the distribution of political and economic power. We accept economic inequality that benefits all, but we will insist on political equality. We will reject Mill's suggestion that the educated should have more votes. How do we reconcile insisting on political equality with accepting economic inequality? How is equal political power to be made consistent with unequal economic power? The urgency of this dilemma varies according to the degree that economic power confers political power.

Not all economic advantages confer disproportionate political power. At one time, it was possible to imagine a world of politically equal smallholders, each in possession of, say, 40 acres and a mule, each doing better or worse depending upon their effort, ingenuity, and (inescapably) luck. The Industrial Revolution swept that world away as technologies made efficiencies of scale possible, bringing into being "the means of production." In our world, a factory owner not only has the capital and incentive to lobby for political favors, but also the power to frustrate democratic decisions by shifting production elsewhere. Economic inequality today generates political inequality unless – somehow – politics can be insulated from economic power.

Insulation of politics from money is unlikely to be enough, even though it will always be necessary. We arrive at "the property question": would it be reasonable to propose allowing private ownership of society's means of production if they could safely be held as our joint property? If we agree to conceive political society as a fair cooperative system for mutual benefit, the answer must be No: these assets are such that private ownership inevitably endows the owner with inordinate political power.

If we dislike this conclusion, and to avoid it would try to conceive of political society some other way – what way is that?

The liberal democratic socialism this book has argued for is secure only if public ownership of the means of production is established as a solemn constitutional guarantee. It has to be as solid as the English monarchy's subservience to Parliament, or as the first amendment to the U.S. Constitution's guarantee of freedom of speech. Even a documentary constitution is, admittedly, no better than a paper guarantee unless it has the support of a solidaristic political culture. The necessary culture will be hospitable to soloists but it cannot be "soloistic" itself. It asks the soloist to let her heart, like Dr. Seuss's Grinch's, grow a little – not necessarily *three* sizes, but at least this one.

Socialism rests ultimately on the realistic hope that growing up in a thriving, supportive, and conspicuously fair society will expand the soloist's affective connections, and she will form an emotional bond to the political society she had no real choice but to join. "Civic friendship" is the term often used to capture this idea. It is a useful one despite the fact that being "forced to be friends" sounds at first as cringeworthy as Rousseau's "being forced to be free."

Civic friendship seldom manifests itself in the kind of feeling that wells up among campers huddled around the campfire, or even among players across the poker table. Civic friends almost never meet up. Civic friends discover each other vicariously, through the common habits they acquire in accessing the means of production that are their joint property. They take quiet pride in the public works they rely upon from day to day, such as a national healthcare system that is free at the point of service, a public transportation system that affordably connects whole communities, or magnificent national parks that belong to everyone.

Civic friends signal their connection to each other, indirectly, in public discourse that appeals to a shared sense of justice, and by their readiness to disapprove and denounce conspicuous injustices, especially those committed in the name of the political society to which the soloist – perhaps now pridefully – belongs. Civic friendship matures among soloists who develop a sensitivity to smaller injustices, and an impatience with subpar official performance. This is how a social contract can cultivate and fortify, even as it presupposes, a solidaristic culture that reconciles the soloist to her social world.

Afterword

Socialism is an idea with a long history: one of millennia, not mere centuries. Even so, after the fall of the Berlin Wall in 1989 and until recently, socialism was widely dismissed as a dead letter. Nevertheless, it is back. Its specter today haunts not only Europe (as Marx and Engels wrote in 1848), Asia, and Africa, but South and even North America. Its reputation as a discussable ideal has been restored. Its potency as a political program has risen (and fluctuated) with the fortunes of figures like Bernie Sanders in the U.S. and Jeremy Corbyn in the U.K. Is this merely a transitory "renaissance faire," a fad destined to fade again as political reality sets in? Or is it evidence that there are durable ideas at the core of socialism, whose association with totalitarianism, violence, and economic underperformance had led many to conclude that it could not survive the advent of neoliberalism and "the end of history"?

The answer to these questions depends on whether or not there are good reasons for people generally to embrace socialism. Socialism is typically introduced as a critique of capitalism, and advocated as the cure to the ails of capitalist societies. This approach has better prospects of success when capitalist countries are in crisis, wages are stagnant, and the upper economic classes are appropriating an increasing share of social wealth. Those who would be better off under socialism of course have a good reason to endorse it. But what of those who would be worse off (as some surely would)? Socialism means abolishing private property in the means of production, including the highly profitable "commanding heights" of financialized economies. Those who would be deprived of the advantages of private property in the means of production have no reason to accept socialism. In fact, they seem to have reason to oppose it.

Can those who believe they would be better off personally without socialism be persuaded otherwise? They might be, if socialists could shift to the perspective of the social contract tradition initiated by Grotius and Hobbes, and taken up by Locke and Rousseau. To succeed, socialists must attend closely to the original, Hobbesian concern for *a stable peace*. Socialism is commonly identified as a development of the three demands of the bourgeois French Revolution of 1789: *Liberté, Egalité, Fraternité*. The central difficulty inherent in socialist doctrine is commonly conceived in terms of reconciling modern liberty with equality and fraternity. This book has been an effort to establish that the most fundamental value of political society is, as Hobbes realized, stability, and the fundamental question of political philosophy is how to stably realize the three values of liberty, equality, and fraternity in societies that exhibit a fundamental, irresolvable plurality of different conceptions of the good.

Although socialist ideas have a long lineage, they came to prominence in the context of industrialization. As Axel Honneth has pointed out, socialism's coming of age during the Industrial Revolution shaped it in certain ways. Most significantly, socialism came to be understood as principally a response to capitalism, and to represent the interests of the vast class of people who owned no or little capital, and had to survive by the sale of their labor power. This industrial proletariat is defined by the wage relation, in which workers sell their labor power to the owners of capital in exchange for a subsistence and access to the means of production, which the capitalist class owns.

This relation was seen as inherently exploitative, in that the surplus value created by the proletariat is appropriated by the capitalist class. By taking ownership of the means of production, the proletariat would capture the just return to its investment of labor. Management of the means of production would be taken over by the workers themselves, shop by shop, and decisions would be made democratically. The two contending classes would merge into one, the victorious proletariat. The state with its apparatus of ministers, police, and courts would wither away, having lost its raison d'être, which is to defend private property in the means of production.

This "economic" conception of socialism is associated with the work of Karl Marx and Friedrich Engels. It found expression in the October 1917 revolution in Russia; but with the dissolution of the Soviet Union in 1991, it appeared to have tipped itself into the dustbin of history. Although the economic conception can be criticized in various ways, this book has been an effort to respond to problems that arise under these three headings: Politics, Class, and Justice.

Politics. Marx and Marxists were skeptical about the possibility of achieving socialism by piecemeal or gradual political reforms. "*Bernsteinism*" was the epithet for those parliamentary socialists who believed otherwise. Although parliamentary measures might be expedient tactically, the advent of socialism would be revolutionary and would sweep away all existing political institutions. No blueprint for socialist institutions was furnished – for the construction of socialism was a task entrusted to a social class, the proletariat. The institutions of a realized socialism cannot be designed beforehand. They will grow out of the existing organization of production and they will be democratic, but – beyond that – little more could be said. It did not work itself out easily in practice. Lenin wrote:

> We must learn to combine the "public meeting" democracy of the working people – turbulent, surging, overflowing its banks like a Spring flood – with *iron discipline* while at work, with *unquestioning obedience* to the will of a single person, the Soviet leader, while at work.

> We have not yet learned to do this. (Lenin 1975: 456)

Common experience teaches us that discussion must come to an end at some point before effective action can be taken, and that cooperative action often requires leadership. Finding the right alloy of democracy and discipline is not impossible; but before it could be learned in Russia, the dictatorship of the soviets (i.e., the local councils) yielded to Communist Party dictatorship and, by 1928 (or earlier), democracy within the Party itself had been extinguished. The mere promise that "it will be more democratic next time" is not enough. Socialism has to reconceive itself as a theory of democratic politics.

Class. Marxian socialism conceives human history as a story of class struggle. Accordingly, humans are regarded primarily as members of contending social classes defined by their relations to the means of production. Socialist economic theory crystallized at a period when "Manchester capitalism" (Honneth 2017: 52) was the salient form of economic organization. Trade unionism grew more-or-less inevitably from the shop-floor experience, in which multitudes of workers cooperated under a single roof for long hours, answering ultimately to an owner, whose speech, dress, and demeanor marked him as a cut above them. Inside and outside the factory gates, the conspicuousness of class distinctions in Victorian England encouraged the idea of class unity and identity.

The revolutionary socialists of the nineteenth century were sure that industrial capitalism had sealed this identity, and that proletarians would feel this fellowship as their primary bond, rather than nation or religion. This faith was tested but not shaken by the capitulation of parliamentary socialists, who voted to fund their respective national armies at the outbreak of World War I. The proletariat, despite its betrayal by the parliamentarians who presumed to represent it, would see that this imperialist war was for the capitalists. Lenin seems never to have accepted that working people might place national sympathy above class-consciousness in their scale of values:

> When an English workers' delegation visited me ... and I told them that every decent English worker should desire the defeat of the English government, they understood nothing. They made faces that I think even the best photograph could not capture. They simply could not get into their heads the truth that in the interests of world revolution, workers must wish the defeat of their government. (Quoted in Krausz 2015: 301)

The solidarity of the working class was never as strong as socialists have supposed. Nor was patriotism as weak. Of his British Labour Party, Clement Attlee is quoted as having said, "When we are returned to power we want to put in the statute book an act which will make our people citizens of the world before they are citizens of this country" (cf. Attlee 1937). Yet, when Labour finally achieved their first ever parliamentary majority and formed a government in 1945, it was on the basis of a strong patriotic appeal to common sacrifice and duty. National solidarity was a powerful element of its success in establishing a Labour government (1945–51) that not only avowed liberal democratic socialism, but came remarkably close to achieving it. Socialism fails to take people as they see themselves if it supposes they will recognize themselves as proletarians first, or as world-citizens first.

Justice. Capitalism makes for winners and losers. But so what? There are winners and losers in any fair competition; and, without competition, society stagnates and individual liberty suffocates. In a world of scarcity, there is always a struggle for survival. Capitalism freed millions from feudal bondage, making it possible for them to bargain to work for whomever they pleased, or to work for themselves, and perhaps become bosses themselves. Marx was leery of stating straight out that a freely bargained wage relation in a capitalistic economy was unjust. But he took care to show how the surplus value made possible by the wage relation gets appropriated one-sidedly, and accrues to the capitalist. This is exploitation, but Marx also recounted the history of how nineteenth-century capitalists used the law to force the English peasantry off the land and into the ranks of an industrial army at the service of the owner class. *Prior* injustices forced the landless to submit to the wage relation on unequal terms.

The theory of the exploitative nature of the wage relation served as the core of socialism's theory of justice, from the founding of the Second International in 1864 at least until the dissolution of the Soviet Union in 1991. But what if that theory is irreparably flawed? It is hard to accept that *every* bargain between one willing to sell their labor power and one willing to pay what is demanded for it is per se unjust. The Marxian theory of exploitation delivers what John Roemer calls "false positives," that is, verdicts of "unjust!" in cases in which that verdict seems misplaced. Moreover, even where the means of production are owned in common, unjust distributions of advantages can still occur. This means that Marxian theory, viewed as an account of distributive justice, also gives some "false negatives" (see Roemer 2017 and also Miller 1990: 196). If socialism understands itself as a struggle against injustice then it has somehow to unshackle itself from the idea that an entirely transaction-specific theory of justice can be correct or complete.

Where to? I have summarized the shortcomings of

socialist theory, as manifested under the three headings of Politics, Class, and Justice. There are noticeable connections. Socialist theory so emphasizes the organization of economic life that the organization of political life tends to be ignored. A political constitution cannot reasonably be expected simply to emerge from a socialist economy – much less can the state be expected simply to wither away once its historical role plays out. Insouciance about this might – only *might* – have made more sense if, in reality, there were a solidary proletarian class whose practical consciousness would forge the necessary political forms, maintain them, and discard them should they no longer serve. But there is no such consciousness. People regard themselves as having diverse identities, associated with and defined by a multiplicity of social roles. Although it may have been forgivable in 1920 to think working people of the world would spontaneously embrace one another in common cause, it is not now.

Lastly, socialists have learned that injustices are not all of a piece, but that does not mean that socialism can proceed without a theory of justice. In fact, it means that not only is a theory of justice demanded, so also is an account of how and why justice mandates socialism. As David Miller argued, on the eve of the collapse of the Soviet Union:

> Many socialists ... attack this or that feature of capitalism, and "socialism" becomes simply a compilation of negatives (no exploitation, no war, no environmental destruction, no subordination of women, etc., etc.). No attempt is made to integrate these undoubtedly desirable aims into some coherent account of the economics and politics of an alternative system. But whatever the justification for such a stance on the part of Marx himself, faced as he was with some of the wilder fantasies of the Utopian socialists, it is no longer either intellectually defensible or politically advantageous to maintain it. Socialism is no longer an unsullied ideal; *faute de mieux*, people will identify it with

the unattractive form of statism that has emerged over the last half-century in Eastern Europe. (1990: 6)

Rehabilitating an ideal means engaging in moral argumentation on its behalf. If talk of injustice involved no more than "bourgeois moralizing," then it is impossible to understand what the socialist project was ever for.

Once socialists accept the obvious demand that socialism produce and defend a theory of justice, they can draw on a wider fund of resources than they can if they restrict themselves to thought that is more central to the socialist tradition. As reviewed above, the Marxian tradition has restricted itself to constrained conceptions of politics, class, and justice. Once the task of designing just political institutions is taken up, socialists can learn to appreciate and turn to use the efforts of the whole tradition of political philosophy: not simply to differentiate socialism, but to work out an attractive housing for it. This book has been an attempt to contribute to the re-ignition of this centuries-spanning effort.

References and Recommended Reading

Abroghati, Reed (2019) "How Apple Uses Its App Store to Copy the Best Ideas," *Washington Post*, September 5, 2019, at https://www.washingtonpost.com/technology/2019/09/05/how-apple-uses-its-app-store-copy-best-ideas (last accessed November 13, 2020).

Allen, Douglas W. (2019) "Giving Away an Empire: Establishing Property Rights Through Coordinated Land Grants," *Journal of Law and Economics* 62: 251–79.

Anderson, Elizabeth (2017) *Private Government: How Employers Rule Our Lives (and Why We Don't Talk About It)*. Princeton: Princeton University Press.

Attlee, C. R. (1937) *The Labour Party in Perspective*. London: Left Book Club.

Bruenig, Matt (2018) *Social Wealth Fund for America*. People's Policy Project.

Boyd, David R. (2019) "Norway: End of Mission Statement of the United Nations Special Rapporteur on Human Rights and the Environment," at https://www.ohchr.org/EN/NewsEvents/Pages/DisplayNews.aspx?NewsID=25032&LangID=E (last accessed November 11, 2020).

Christman, Matt (2020) "Musings," *Chapo Trap House* No. 426, June 8, 2020.

Cringely, Robert X. (1992) *Accidental Empires*. New York: Addison-Wesley.

Cohen, G. A. (2009) *Why Not Socialism?* Princeton: Princeton University Press.

Edmundson, William A. (2017) *John Rawls: Reticent Socialist*. Cambridge: Cambridge University Press.

Freeman, Samuel (2007) *Rawls*. London: Routledge.

Fried, Barbara (2012) "The Unwritten Theory of Justice: Rawlsian Liberalism versus Libertarianism," in *The Blackwell Companion to Rawls*, ed. Jon Mandle and David Reidy. Oxford: Blackwell.

Friedel, Robert (2010) *A Culture of Improvement: Technology and the Western Millennium*. Cambridge, MA: MIT Press.

Harress, Christopher (2018) "Winning Lottery Ticket for Alabama Waffle House Waitress led to Lawsuit, Kidnapping," *Mobile Real-Time News*, October 24, 2018, at https://www.al.com/news/mobile/2018/10/winning-lottery-ticket-for-alabama-waffle-house-waitress-led-to-lawsuit-kidnapping.html (last accessed September 10, 2020).

Hobbes, Thomas (1651) *Leviathan* (any edition showing 1651 "Head" pagination).

— (1642) *De Cive*, various editions.

Honneth, Axel (2017) *The Idea of Socialism*. Cambridge: Polity Press.

Johnson, Simon (2019) "Egalitarian Sweden Getting More Unequal as Tax Cuts Help the Rich," *Reuters*, April 9, 2019, at https://www.reuters.com/article/us-sweden-equality-analysis/egalitarian-sweden-getting-more-unequal-as-tax-cuts-help-the-rich-idUSKCN1RL0WU (last accessed September 25, 2020).

Knight, Frank H. (1935) *The Ethics of Competition and Other Essays*. New York: Harper & Bros.

Krausz, Tamás (2015) *Reconstructing Lenin: An Intellectual Biography*. New York: Monthly Review Press.

Lenin, V. I. (1975) *The Lenin Anthology*, ed. Robert C. Tucker. New York: W. W. Norton.

Lincoln, Abraham (1953) *The Collected Works of Abraham Lincoln*, 8 vols, ed. Roy P. Basler. New Brunswick: Rutgers University Press.

Marx, Karl (1867) *Capital*, vol. I, various editions.

Miller, David (1990) *Market, State, and Community: Theoretical Foundations of Market Socialism*. Oxford: Clarendon Press.

Mosey, Chris (1982) "Sweden's Abba Sings the Blues ... And Socialist Plans Cause Private Industry to Join the Chorus," *The Christian Science Monitor*, September 1, 1982, at https://www.csmonitor.com/layout/set/print/1982/0901/090150.html (last accessed September 12, 2020).

Nozick, Robert (1974) *Anarchy, State, and Utopia*. New York: Basic Books.

Pilon, Mary (2015) *The Monopolists: Obsession, Fury, and the Scandal Behind the World's Favorite Board Game*. London: Bloomsbury.

Pistor, Katherina (2019) *The Code of Capital: How Law Creates Wealth and Inequality*. Princeton: Princeton University Press.

Rawls, John (1999a) *A Theory of Justice*, revised edition. Cambridge MA: Harvard University Press.

— (1999b) *Collected Papers*, ed. Samuel Freeman. Cambridge, MA: Harvard University Press.

— (2001) *Justice as Fairness: A Restatement*. Cambridge MA: Harvard University Press.

Roemer, John E. (1994) *A Future for Socialism*. Cambridge MA: Harvard University Press.

— (2017) "Socialism Revised," *Philosophy & Public Affairs* 45(3): 261–315.

Rousseau, Jean-Jacques (1755) *Second Discourse on the Origin of Inequality*, various editions.

Thomas, Alan (2016) *A Republic of Equals*. Oxford: Oxford University Press.

Wendt, Fabian (2018) *Authority*. Cambridge: Polity Books.

Wilkinson, Richard, and Kate Pickett (2010) *The Spirit Level: Why Greater Equality Makes Societies Stronger*. New York: Bloomsbury.

Witt, April (2018) "He Won Powerball's $314 Million Jackpot. It Ruined His Life," *The Washington Post*, October 23, 2018, at https://www.washingtonpost.com/history/2018/10/24/jack-whittaker-powerball-lottery-winners-life-was-ruined-after-m-jackpot (last accessed September 12, 2020).

Index